What practising managers say abc

Few managers have the time to seriously
philosophy or theory. However, most will a
guidelines that, if applied, will certainly hel
where everyone enjoys a sense of value anu snareu purpose. i iuunu uiis
book to be simple, practical and extremely useful as a quick guide to what is
important in today's business environment.

Glyn Ashley
Founder Chairman, Dubai Quality Group, United Arab Emirates.

Dan has yet again produced a concise, step by step approach to managing in
today's ever changing environment. Make it a must for your managers.

Steve Jones
Director, Asset Management, Western Australian Police Services.

A succinct summary of the modern day managers toolkit for self
and team improvement. This will be a great reference source of practical
actions for all managers and is an invaluable guide for those new to the
role of managing people.

Kevin Maitland
Senior Manager Subiaco Group, Commonwealth Bank of Australia

Excellent. A trip back to reality for managers entangled in a web of fads
and new organisation initiatives.

Naomi Brown
Human Resources Manager, Bulk Water and Wastewater Division, Water Corporation

As a typical hands on manager of a business, I consider myself a sceptic of
meetings, seminars and 'professional management practices', etc. but I found
"You lead, they'll follow" surprisingly succinct and easy to read. A definite
inclusion in the office library for easy and frequent reference.

Frank van der Worm
Director, Granwood Flooring.

This book is both an inspiration and an amusement. It should be compulsory
reading for anybody who is responsible for trying to get the best out of people.

Rod Hooper
Partner, Lewis Blyth and Hooper.

"You lead, they'll follow" has the potential to transform an ordinary, struggling
business into a dynamic, productive enterprise, with an unlimited future.

Dr J P O'Shea
Cardiologist, Fremantle Hospital.

No jargon, no complex theories, and no pretence. Just sensible and straight forward ideas to help managers succeed at work. Unlike the theoretical reliance of many management texts, this book is a practical aid in the 'real world' of work.

Peter Mott
Executive Director, Corporate Services, Fremantle Hospital.

This is an excellent book. Written in an understandable everyday format which can be easily applied by managers and supervisors.

Eric Baines
Manager Human Resources, Totalisator Agency Board.

A highly credible and essential reference book that should be kept in sight on your desk top so that the next people problem can be quickly turned into your people's solution.

David Longmuir
General Manager, Operations Support, John Holland Construction Asia

I read the book in one go, which is a great indicator of it's interest and simplicity. The authors have successfully sidestepped the temptation of gross verbosity when writing about management principles. The messages are clear and concise and they relate directly to real people and workplaces.

Don Beard
Human Resource Systems Co-ordinator, Western Power Corporation

No matter what the competence level is of today's manager, we all suffer from a lack of recall when it comes to the best and simplest solutions to our complex problems.
What a great toolbox "You lead, they'll follow" will be to have on hand!

Steve McInerney
State Sales and Marketing Manager,WA, Smorgon ARC.

What a great checklist for managers in helping them to build a healthy and positive working relationship with employees.
Well worth a space on my bookshelf!

Pamela Lewis
Employee Relations Manager, Town of Kwinana

This book is an invaluable inventory of practical management guidance.

Kim Clark
Manager, Lower Great Southern Regional Health Service.

The book provides an excellent checklist of issues to consider in the key day-to-day activities that face a manager.

Dr Bryan Jenkins
Chief Executive Officer, Department of Environmental Protection.

You lead, they'll follow

How to inspire, lead and manage people. Really.

Daniel Kehoe and Stephen Godden

Cartoons by Dean Alston

Bentley Kehoe Consulting Group
Perth, Western Australia.

First published in Australia 1998

Reprinted 1999

Published by BKC Pty Ltd
Trading as Bentley Kehoe Consulting Group
82 Simper Street, Wembley
Western Australia. 6014.

Design and layout by Natalie Cuss
Printed and bound in Australia by Lamb Print
Robertson Street, Perth
Western Australia. 6000.

To order "You lead, they'll follow"
Phone: +(618) 9284 0039
Fax: +(618) 9284 0041
E-mail: msi@iexpress.net.au

About this book

As we move into the 21st century, life appears to become more and more complex - the demands for change ever increasing. What people are looking for are ways to simplify the complex - to make sense of their world.

This is no less evident in our worklives. Employees are regularly bombarded with the latest fad, theory or management tool. No wonder the longer serving employees adopt the view, "this too shall pass" as they brace themselves for the latest program to sweep through their workplace.

The management of people is complex because people are complex. Yet successful people managers do simple, basic things. If you compare the styles of effective managers, you will find common characteristics - they do and say similar things regardless of the type of industry in which they work.

I have spent nearly 20 years discussing and recording how some 3,500 managers manage - what they actually do and say to deal with the complex issues and problems they face in their daily worklife.

These managers or supervisors or team leaders come from a diverse range of industry sectors - mining, finance, insurance, manufacturing, oil, energy, printing, food processing, construction, health, education, hospitality, tourism, telecommunications, electronic, post and retail. They also include managers from various public sector utilities and agencies at local, state and federal level.

I believe a critical goal for a manager is to win and maintain the respect of his or her people. With that respect a manager can achieve much. Without that respect, a manager is doomed.

Fundamental to this are dignity and self-worth. In their dealings with their people, the successful manager tries to say and do things which enhance the sense of dignity and self-worth of their people.

Being a manager is not a popularity contest. You are required to make hard decisions which will not always meet the wants of all of your people. But the complex task of managing people becomes more productive, much easier and more rewarding when you have the respect of your people

"You lead, they'll follow" shows you what real managers say and do in real situations with real people to be successful.

Daniel Kehoe

About the authors

Dan Kehoe has been designing and facilitating management training and development workshops since 1979. In that time he has worked with over 3,500 managers ranging from chief executives to frontline managers.

He has worked with managers in all states of Australia, in Indonesia, Malaysia, Dubai (United Arab Emirates) and the United States of America.

As a management consultant, he has spent thousands of hours listening to and discussing with practising managers how to solve the real life issues and problems related to managing people.

He is a director of Bentley Kehoe Consulting Group (which he established in 1987) and M•A•P•P™ Systems International based in Perth, Western Australia.

He is the creator and designer of the M•A•P•P™ System - a new and innovative management process for improving any aspect of organisation performance. He is also the designer of the Management in Action Workshops which are based on "You lead, they'll follow".

He has a Masters Degree in Management Science and a Graduate Diploma in the field of applied behavioural science.

He is a member of the Institute of Management Consultants and has been awarded the grading of CMC - Certified Management Consultant.

Steve Godden has worked in the management consulting field since 1992.

During this time he has worked with managers and staff from over 200 different organisations across more than 15 different industry sectors.

Steve started his working life as a teacher and spent over 20 years living and working in many different locations throughout Western Australia both in the classroom and as a school administrator. In the latter role, he had the additional challenge of not only managing staff, but parents and children too. He has a keen interest in adult education, management practices and professional development with the purpose of improving organisational efficiency through staff development.

In 1997 Steve wrote, with Dan Kehoe, the popular book "Tips for Teachers and School Administrators". The book has been sold in England, Ireland, Scotland, Wales, New Zealand and Singapore as well as Australia.

Steve has had significant input into the design of the M•A•P•P™ System - a new and innovative management process which he has adapted to suit the Education scenario. He has implemented the system into some 27 organisations.

He is a qualified Lead Auditor in the Quality Assurance area and has a great interest in the link between quality, management and employee behaviour.

His qualifications include a Bachelor of Education with a major in Computer Education.

About Dean Alston

Dean Alston is one of Australia's greatest cartoonists. He is the editorial cartoonist for The West Australian newspaper.

His keen and intelligent insight into the human condition combined with his artistic skills have won him over 15 national awards for cartooning. He is a seriously funny man.

Quotations

Many of the quotations used in "You lead, they'll folllow" are sourced from:
- "The Manager's Book of Quotations" by Lewis D. Eigen and Johnathon P. Seigel, Amacon 1989.
- "The International Thesaurus of Quotations" compiled by Rhoda Thomas Tripp, Penguin Reference Books 1976.

Both of these books are highly recommended as sources of quotations for inspiraton, humour, wisdom, practical advice, writing and public speaking.

Acknowledgments

My thoughts about managing and being managed have been shaped by a number of people during my worklife. First and foremost, the late Gwynn Gibbons, a brave, intelligent, wise and sensitive man who saw something others didn't, took a risk and gave me an opportunity. Brian McSweeney who brought out the best in me. Mary Ballantine and Elizabeth Mulrennan for their intelligence, practical wisdom, great humour and counsel (Liz). Antony Power who dared to do things who also took a risk and gave me a fantastic opportunity. Dr Peter Saul for his great intelligence and humour who taught me much about managing and management consulting. Sally Jardine for her wisdom, compassion, great fun and joie de vivre. Helen Crossing for her intelligent observations about organisations and people and for her spirit. Steve Godden for his patience, humour, dedication, high quality thinking, counsel and the constant reminder that there's more than one way to skin a cat.

To Yasmin Naglazas for her never ending love and support and to my long time friends Dennis Smith, Michael Kehoe, Sherry Abrahmsen, and my mother, Carmel, all of whom helped me out when the going got tough. A thank you, in particular, to Bruce Cherry for his page-by-page analysis and Terrie O'Shea for her general impressions of the manuscript. All the 3,500 or so managers, supervisors and team leaders over the years who have shared the highs and lows, the frustrations and the successes, the insights and learnings about the greatest challenge facing the manager - managing the world's potentially greatest asset - our workforce.

Daniel Kehoe

With love and appreciation to my immediate
family Kevin, Carmel, Mary, Michael, Anne, Nicole and Joel
Daniel Kehoe

To my beautiful girls, Debbie, Brodie and Katie,
and in loving memory of my mother Daphne and my father Jeff.
Stephen Godden

CONTENTS

Changing Your Management Style
- Can a leopard change its spots?   6

Team Building
- How does your team rate?   8
- Team effectiveness assessment tool   10
- Team values   12

Assertiveness
- My rights are your rights. Right?   14

Behaviour
- Vive la difference   16

Change
- Preparing the ground   18
- The meat in the sandwich   20
- Remember the good old days   22

Changing Behaviour
- Send reinforcements, we're going to advance   24

Client Supplier Relationship
- Once removed   26
- Customer's last stand   28
- Stand and deliver   30

Coaching
- Tell and show   32

Communication
- In one ear and out the other   34
- Curiosity killed the cat, information brought it back   36
- The mushroom syndrome   38
- What we have here is a failure to communicate   40
- Read my lips   42
- Rudyard Kipling's six wise men   44

Complaints
- Squeaky wheels need oiling (or replacing)   46

Conflict Resolution
- Lose the battle - win the war   48
- Winning isn't everything   50

Consultative Planning
- Two heads are better than one   52

Continuous Improvement
- We've always done it this way   54

Corporate Loyalty
- What do they really think?   56

Cost Reduction
- Count every cent - every cent counts   58

1

Counselling	• Choices and consequences	60
	• Switch off and switch on	62
	• You can do better than that	64
Creating New Business	• The world is your oyster	66
Creativity and Innovation	• Can't see the wood for the trees	68
Customer Perceptions	• Standin' on the outside, lookin' In	70
Customer Service	• Opportunity only knocks once	72
	• Moments of truth	74
Decision Making	• There's more than one way to skin a cat	76
Delegation	• Delegation not abdication	78
Fear	• Fear and loathing in the workplace	80
	• Is the glass half full or half empty?	82
Feedback	• Don't say don't	84
Grievances	• Good grief!	86
Induction	• First impressions stick	88
	• A good start	90
Interdepartmental Co-operation	• 'Us' versus 'them'	92
Interpersonal Relationships	• What you put out you get back	94
	• Walk the talk	96
Job Description	• Resume the position	98
Job Interviews	• Any questions?	100
	• Round peg, square hole	102
	• Sell yourself or else	104
	• Can you judge a book by its cover?	106
Leadership	• Captain, my captain	108
	• Nothing stays up without support	110
Listening	• The lights are on but nobody's home	112

CONTENTS

Management Effectiveness	• It takes guts, but ask them	114
Management Information Systems	• Fact or fiction?	116
Meetings	• A necessary evil	118
	• Meetings, meetings, meetings, and more bloody meetings	120
	• You can make a difference	122
	• Silence is compliance	124
Mentoring	• A voyage of self discovery	126
	• Lead from behind	128
	• Let the penny drop	130
Mission	• The big picture	132
Morale	• Skill is nil without will	134
Motivating Staff	• What cheeses me off	136
Negotiation	• If you show me yours, I'll show you mine	138
	• Give away the wool, not the sheep	140
Perceptions	• Beauty is in the eye of the beholder	142
	• Why don't they do what they're supposed to do?	144
Performance Appraisal	• As good as it gets	146
	• Was it good for you too?	148
	• Tell it as it really is	150
Performance Counselling	• One bad apple.....	152
Performance Indicators	• Lead and lag	154
Performance Management	• Tend the garden, pick the flowers	156
Performance Problems	• Prevention is better than cure	158
	• Nip it in the bud	160
	• Say what?	162
Persuasion	• Something on your mind?	164

Politics	• Make no enemies	166
Praise	• You stupid bloody idiot!	168
Problem Solving	• Get the monkeys off your back	170
	• Treat the cause, not the symptoms	172
Project Management	• A project manager's checklist	174
Public Speaking	• As ye sow so shall ye reap	176
	• Free sex	178
	• Very interesting	180
Reading	• Read and digest	182
	• Knowledge is power	184
Recognition and Feedback	• Ask me no questions and I'll tell you no lies	186
	• Damned with faint praise	188
Respect	• Never trust a skinny cook	190
Role Clarification	• Don't look at me....	192
	• Where does that buck stop?	194
Role of Frontline Manager	• Back to front	196
Safety	• Think safety first, second and third!	198
	• Safety is no accident you have to prepare for it	200
Sales	• Accentuate the positives, eliminate the negatives	202
	• If I....... would you....?	204
	• Managing sales performance 1	206
	• Managing sales performance 2	208
	• Hit and miss	210
	• Always ask for the business	212
	• Gee... I hadn't thought of that	214
	• Slimy might sell, but it doesn't stick	216
Strategic Planning	• If you don't know where you're going, it doesn't matter how you get there	218
Stress Management	• Dead man walking	220
	• Mind over matter	222
	• Relaxevous	224

CONTENTS

Team Participation   • Know thyself   226

Technology   • The point of no return   228

Time Management   • You can't manage time   230
• Time demand analysis   232
• Time saving tips   234
• Where does time go?   236
• Waste not want not   238
• It takes two to tango   240

Tolerance   • Patience is a virtue   242

Training   • We must keep topping up the well   244
• Awareness precedes all learning   246
• You only play as you train   248
• Plan before you train   250
• Training is important but we can't stop production   252
• Inspect the expected   254
• No pain, no gain   256

Vision   • The mission is missin'   258

Workload Overload   • The straw that broke the camel's back   260

Writing   • The penis mightier than the sword   262
• Write right   264

Afterword   • The new way to manage   266
• How to incorporate the philosophy and actions of "You lead, they'll follow" into the culture of your organisation   270
• How to train your managers in the philosophy and actions of "You lead, they'll follow"   271
• Frontline Management initiatives   272

Can a leopard change its spots?

Some managers work in an environment where their level of trust, respect and credibility is already damaged because of their style of managing people. Is it too late to learn? Is it too late to change? Is it too late to win back the trust, respect and credibility?

If your relationship with your people has been damaged by past events and you're happy to maintain that situation - so be it. If however you are of the view that it's never too late, then this book will show you hundreds of ways to turn that situation around. But it won't happen overnight.

There is only one way to begin to win back the trust, respect and credibility. That is to speak honestly with your people about the current situation and what you want to do about it and why. You are probably going to have to eat some 'humble pie'. To pretend that the past hasn't happened will be folly. Your credibility in changing your style will be lost immediately. It's just a matter of acknowledging the past.

Here is a range of things you might say at a meeting with your team or individually to your team members. (Say these in your own style, but don't change the meaning of the message you want to convey):

- "I guess it is common knowledge that my relationship with some of you (all of you) could be improved."
- "I'm aware that some things have happened in the past that have put a strain on the relationship I have with some of you (all of you)."
- "I'm aware that over the years we've had some differences of opinion that have upset various people."
- "It's no secret that there is bad blood between me and a few of you (all of you). There have been a few things that, with hindsight, could have been handled better by both you and me."
- "We have a couple of choices. We can stay in the past and continue as we are or we can learn from our mistakes and make some changes to improve things for everybody."
- "I'm willing to admit I made some mistakes and to learn from them and move forward. I'd like to try over the next few weeks to change a few things about my approach. But to make any overall improvement I need you to help. It has to be a two way thing. Is that fair?"
- "I'm going to try and do some new, different and better things to improve the current situation. I don't expect to win you over overnight, but I would like you to know that I'll be trying. How do you feel about giving it a go?"

How does your team rate?

How effective is your team? Here is an assessment tool you can use on your team or work group. Before using it, decide if both you and your team have the maturity to deal with the consequences. Also decide if you are prepared to act on the results. To do this exercise and then do nothing after will seriously damage your credibility. You will need to have a healthy self-esteem and be willing to see criticism as an opportunity for improvement.

Explain what you are doing and why and ask staff to assist you to make sure that we are working as effectively as we can as a team and that team morale is as good as it can be. Tell them what you plan to do with their evaluations and what you propose to do with the results. Agree with the team whether to keep it confidential or not. If the decision is to keep it confidential, re-think whether or not the team has the maturity to conduct its own evaluation or whether or not there is a fear of repercussions.

Tell them that as the group or team leader, ultimate accountability for team performance, team morale and team effectiveness rests with you, but that without their co-operation you can do little to improve things if improvements are required. Ask them to be honest, fair and balanced in their evaluations.

Firstly, check out the assessment tool and suggested rating scale on pages 9 and 10. Then come back and read these guidelines and considerations about improving team performance and team morale using this assessment tool:

The assessment tool contains 60 items relating to team effectiveness. There are others that you could think of and may wish to add, but if most of these items are being well managed within the team you will have a very effective team.
The optimum score possible using our suggested rating scale is 420 - the perfect score for the ideal team. Now if your score for your team's effectiveness is somewhat less than the perfect score - don't panic. The ideal score of 420 is a target to aim for which realistically no team will ever achieve, but it does give you something to strive for.

- Here are some benchmarks for comparing your team score :

60 - 120   **Frankly - a lot of people find renewal in early retirement.**
121 - 180   **Huh? Teamwork you say. What's that?**
181 - 240   **Phew! You've got a hell of a lot of work to do.**
241 - 300   **Well. At least you can see the light at the end of the tunnel.**
301 - 360   **Not bad. Not bad, at all. You've got a pretty good team there.**
361 - 420   **Congratulations. You have a fantastic team.**

- Involve all team members in conducting the evaluation.
- Combine the individual total scores to work out the average total score.
- Combine the individual scores for each item to work out the average score for each item.
- Make a note of items where there is a wide difference in individual scores, e.g. 1,2,6,5,3,1,6,2,5. Discuss why there is such a variation in scores at the team meeting. Ask people to explain their reasons for their rating.
- To begin with, focus on the 5 items which have the lowest average score.
- Discuss with the team what has to happen to improve these things. Agree what things you will do and what things team members will do. Emphasise that for you to make improvements you are going to need their support and co-operation. And vice versa.
- Draw up a list of actions to be implemented by you and/or the team members describing the actions, by whom, with whom and by when.
- Agree to meet in, say, two weeks to review the progress with this list of actions.
- Create an expectation that all team members, where relevant, will be expected to discuss verifiable examples of how they have acted to begin these improvements.
- At this team meeting, always lead off by discussing verifiable examples of what you have done. Then ask others to discuss their examples.
- Keep repeating this process every two weeks or so until the team is satisfied that   the first 5 items have been addressed.
- Now focus on the next 5 items with the lowest average score. Check - many of the items are not mutually exclusive, i.e. items may be related to each other. Thus, by improving one item you may also improve another related item. Review if the next 5 lowest items still need improving. If not, choose the next 5 items or whatever that still need improving.
- Continue this process until you conduct your next team evaluation in 6 months.
- Continue the team improvement cycle, as necessary.

Team effectiveness - assessment tool

Below is a suggested rating scale :

1	2	3	4	5	6	7
Strongly Disagree	Disagree	Moderately Disagree	Neutral	Moderately Agree	Agree	Strongly Agree

1. All people are treated equally and without bias.
2. Creativity and innovation are promoted within the team.
3. Everybody works to the agreed standards.
4. Right efforts are acknowledged as much as right results.
5. Work problems and issues are clarified and resolved.
6. I can express any opinion I like without fear of repercussion.
7. What people say is consistent with what they do.
8. Honesty is displayed within the team.
9. People are prepared to listen to what I have to say.
10. Trust is displayed within the team.
11. We provide each other with recognition and feedback.
12. People seldom interrupt others.
13. We frequently clarify what we need and expect from each other.
14. If decisions were made secret ballot, they would be the same as those we currently make.
15. We communicate effectively between team members.
16. We look for ways to assist other members of the team.
17. Everybody is allowed to have a say - no one dominates.
18. We are allowed to question the established systems and practices within the team.
19. We are open to ways to improve our individual performance.
20. Team meetings are effective, worthwhile and looked forward to by the team.
21. We spend time clarifying the objectives of the team.
22. We are all clear on our roles and responsibilities.
23. Our individual goals are the same as the team goals.
24. We get appropriate feedback on team performance.
25. Team efforts and results are acknowledged and recognised.
26. Our team goals are achievable.
27. We have appropriate input into team goals and strategies.
28. Our priorities are clear.
29. We have a clear understanding of what is expected of us on a day to day basis.

30. Members of the team are committed to the team.
31. When things go wrong we look for learnings and solutions, not blame.
32. We participate in relevant decision making and are committed to the implementation.
33. We are flexible and adaptable to changing circumstances.
34. We always act and follow up on decisions made at team meetings.
35. We have a focus on continuous improvement.
36. We all accept that all of us have a part to play in team effectiveness and team morale.
37. Problems and issues are discussed within the team before decisions are made.
38. We know each others' strengths and limitations and work to complement each other.
39. People tend to be constructive rather than destructive.
40. People are prepared to own and discuss errors knowing that this information won't be used against them later.
41. People are prepared to share success and acknowledge their team members.
42. I can do my job properly because other members in the team do their job properly.
43. We are prepared to work with other teams.
44. When the going gets tough, there is a sense of support amongst the team.
45. There are no destructive cliques in our team.
46. Other teams welcome the opportunity to work with us.
47. Team members accept feedback on performance from each other.
48. The team can count on the manager for support.
49. Conflict between team members is resolved fairly and positively.
50. We follow the agreed systems and procedures.
51. People would welcome job rotation within the team.
52. The right people do the right jobs in this team.
53. We evaluate the way we work as a team.
54. People understand the concept of client - supplier relationships within the team and external to the team.
55. The team has the right skills and expertise to get the job done.
56. People understand the roles that other people in the team perform.
57. We have the power to achieve what we are meant to achieve.
58. Our manager represents our views to other management.
59. The role of the leader and manager is respected in the team.
60. People are willing to accept ownership of their actions.

Team values

Every organisation has its own culture - the way we do things. This culture reflects the values of the people who create and implement the policies which govern how the organisation functions. Hopefully, it also reflects the values of the employees who actually perform the various functions and tasks required to implement these policies.

This is an important consideration for a manager. If you want your people to continually strive to improve their performance, it is obviously far better if they want to do that of their own volition. It is extremely difficult to get people to do things which are against their own set of values.

You can't really get people to do something against their will. You can if you continually maintain a threat of punishment, but at what cost? In this situation, people will find ways to sabotage your efforts, they will do things to a low standard, make it a low priority, do it half-heartedly or not do it at all.

Within the organisation culture, a manager can create a sub-culture within the work group or team. In terms of the way we do things within our team, what are the things that team members value that keep them motivated?

Here is a tool a manager can use to check that the team culture is a positive one which encourages optimum team performance.

- Using the 'Team Values' list (or start from scratch and develop your own set of values), ask each team member to select the 10 most important to them.
- Ask them to attach a weight to each value. 10 points to their most important value, 9 points to their next most important value, and so on.
- Collect each team member's top 10 values (including your own) and determine the top 12 values for the team.
- Do this by adding the individual weightings for each value. The value with the highest total weighting is the number one priority value for the team. The value with the second highest total weighting is the number two priority value for the team. And so on.
- Now, working with your team and starting with the number one team value, answer these questions :
  1. What do we need to do more of?
  2. What do we need to do less of?
  3. What do we need to do differently?
  to demonstrate that this value is actually reflected in the ways we do things within our team.
- Agree a list of actions and a process to manage and monitor the implementation of these actions.

TEAM VALUES

- **Open and honest communication**
- **Support for each other**
- **Creativity**
- **Purpose**
- **Trust**
- **Recognition and feedback**
- **Skill sharing and development**
- **Risk taking**
- **Vision**
- **Direction and support**

- **Humour and fun**
- **Respect**
- **Equality**
- **Ethics**
- **Learning**
- **Accountability**
- **Diversity**
- **Shared workload**
- **Conflict resolution**
- **Continuous improvement**

My rights are your rights. Right?

No one would argue that if the United Nations' Universal Bill of Rights was enacted throughout the world, the world would be a far better place. In an enlightened and humane workplace, people too have certain rights.

While there are exceptions, in most situations managers are most effective when they act assertively.

One definition of acting assertively is to act in a way which recognises your rights while at the same time not violating the rights of others. Likewise, aggressive behaviour can be defined as acting in a way which recognises your rights but not the rights of others. And non-assertive behaviour can be defined as acting in a way which denies your rights while allowing the rights of others.

Here is a list of rights you might accord to yourself and to others in the workplace:
The right to
- A safe work environment.
- Have and express my own opinions and feelings.
- Question policies and procedures which appear counter-productive.
- Open and honest communication.
- Work in an environment free of fear.
- Honest feedback on my performance, both negative and positive.
- Be listened to and taken seriously.
- Ask for information which affects how I do my job.
- Be involved in decisions which affect how I do my job.
- Be given opportunities to develop skills.
- Be rewarded fairly for my efforts.
- A clear and concise job description.
- Know by what criteria my performance is judged.
- Know how my performance is viewed.
- Know how the company is performing.
- Challenge unfair industrial relations practices.

You might disagree with some of these rights or believe in other rights not listed here. But whatever you believe about people's rights in the workplace will dictate your management style. It would be a useful exercise to discuss this list of rights with your staff or even develop your own 'Bill of Rights' for your workplace using input from the whole team.

There are some people who argue that people don't have rights as such and that they have to create their own circumstances. Whatever, all would probably agree that the workplace would be a better place if the above conditions existed.

Vive la difference

The late and great Professor Julius Sumner Miller once liked to ask, "Why is it so?" as he challenged our understanding of some scientific law which we usually took for granted without ever really knowing why. A manager will often ask the same question as he or she ponders the behaviour of their staff when they behave in ways which defy common sense or logic. Unfortunately, or probably fortunately, there are no scientific laws which absolutely explain human behaviour.

A manager needs to understand that people behave differently from them for a variety of reasons. No two people have exactly the same psychological make-up or experience the world in the same way. Which is why we need managers.

There are two major variables which influence a person's work behaviour - one, factors inherent to the person and, two, factors external to the person within their work environment.

What are the factors inherent to the person which influence their behaviour?
• Physical and mental health.

- Intelligence.
- Skills and knowledge.
- Attitudes, values, beliefs.
- Prejudices, biases.
- Perceptions.
- Self-esteem.
- Needs.
- Temperament.
- Work experience, etc.

And each of these factors will be different for you and each one of your staff. No two people will have exactly the same perceptions, the same work experience, the same level of skill or knowledge, the same temperament, the same values, etc.

What are the factors external to the person within their work environment which influence their behaviour?
- The culture of the organisation - the way we do things.
- Team dynamics
- The structure of the organisation.
- Office politics.
- The vision, mission, policy and strategy.
- Systems, procedures and work practices
- The actions of others - managers and workmates,
- The physical structures, materials and equipment.
- Laws and regulations.
- Customer expectations.
- Community expectations, etc.

And again everyone's perceptions and understandings of these factors will differ.

Arguably, the factors which have most influence on a person's behaviour are:
- perceptions
- values
- the actions of their workmates
- the actions of their manager.

Preparing the ground

> Observe constantly that all things take place by change,
> and accustom thyself to consider that the nature of the Universe
> loves nothing so much as to change the things which are,
> and to make new things like them.
> **Marcus Aurelias, 121-180**
> *Roman Emperor and Stoic philosopher Meditations*
>
> Many of the obstacles for change which have been attributed to human
> nature are in fact due to the inertia of institutions and to the voluntary
> desire of powerful classes to maintain the existing status.
> **John Dewey, 1859-1952**
> *American philosopher and educator*
> *Encyclopedia of Unified Sciences, 1938*

How often are industrial disputes or a drop in productivity the result of change which is forced upon a protesting workforce? New procedures initiated by management are sometimes totally rejected or are only partially implemented.

It's interesting to ponder that there is still a prevailing thought within boards of directors and within senior management that if employees don't "like it, they can lump it" or get a job somewhere else. Let's face it, there aren't too many boardroom decisions made on the basis of what's best for our employees - in the boardroom, the dollar is God.

Fortunately, there are pockets of enlightenment around where there is a realisation that good profits with a good return on investment to shareholders and fair and caring people management aren't mutually exclusive.

When management is intending to introduce change, the planning process can involve input from the workforce on the best way to bring about the change. After all, it is the workforce which has to actually implement the change. They are more likely to be committed to the change if they see that their perceptions have been considered.

Here are some questions to consider before trying something new:
- Are resources (time, money, equipment, personnel, information, procedures, etc.) adequate for allowing the change?
- Do others possess the motivation and commitment to bring about the change?
- What are the prevailing perceptions about the intended change?
- Is the change likely to encounter 'closed thinking' or resistance?
- What are the likely obstacles to using new procedures in the minds of the staff?
- Could existing communication channels block implementation of the intended change?
- What organisation or management policies will need to be overcome to allow effective implementation?
- If the new ideas are untried or unproven, will the people responsible for the implementation be willing to take the risks?
- Are there on-going power struggles within the organisation - even if unrelated to the new changes - which might block implementation?
- Are there any people conflicts which might prevent the new procedures from being put into action?
- Is the general climate of the organisation one of co-operation or distrust?
- What are staff perceptions of the need for or the reasons behind the change?
- How will the question "what's in it for me?" be answered?
- To what degree are staff convinced of the need or reasons for change?
- What can be done to reduce the 'fear' perceptions staff may hold concerning the change?
- What support and training will staff need to accommodate the change?
- How will management act to demonstrate real support for the change? How will management show that they too will do new, different and better things as a response to the need for change?

The meat in the sandwich

Middle management have the unenviable task of having to 'keep the peace' at both ends of the organisation. Ensuring that you maintain a loyalty to the organisation while implementing its strategic goals and 'looking after' the staff can be a very difficult thing to do. The aim is to keep the balance while moving forward at the same time.

In effect, you are the buffer zone or conduit depending upon the way you look at it. You buffer the change through facilitation, nurturing, encouraging, rewarding, screening, sifting and supporting. You act as the conduit by channelling, directing, describing, implementing, evaluating, monitoring and communicating. Keeping this balance can be an emotional and physical drain. You have two 'masters' to keep happy. How do you do this?

What to do as the buffer / conduit:

WITH STAFF

- Discuss reasons behind new initiatives.
- Involve them in the planning stages.
- Discuss the strategic goals of the organisation and how they affect their area.
- Explain the benefits of the new initiatives to the organisation and to them.
- Explain what your role is in the process.
- Ask staff how they feel about the new changes and assure them that you will inform senior management.
- Ask for and discuss the reasons behind staff perceptions of changes.
- Point out that while you understand why they are feeling as they are that for the reasons outlined the changes are still to go ahead.
- Ask them if they can think of better ways of doing the same thing without the apparent pain it may be causing.
- Provide training in areas which require new skills for them to do the job.

WITH MANAGEMENT

- Explain how staff are feeling about issues.
- Explain what you are doing to implement the changes.
- Inform them of what support you need from them to help you implement the changes.
- Inform them of staff suggestions about how to implement the change.
- Ask them to respond and provide reasons why staff suggestions are not taken up.
- Discuss the consequences of moving too quickly or too slowly.
- Inform them of the communication requirements of staff.
- Ask them what other things they can suggest that you may not have already done to implement the change.

Remember the good old days

People resist change for a variety of reasons, but they can usually be categorised under one heading - fear. Fear of : the unknown, loss of face, embarrassment, loss of power, loss of control, failure, loss of security, disturbance to their 'comfort zone', inability to adapt, inability to acquire new skills, peer group pressure, an attack on their own personal values, loss of dignity and self-esteem, etc.

While people like routine and habit, not all people resist change. Many welcome and embrace change because they view it as exciting, different and a sign of progress.

By eliminating or modifying fear-based perceptions, the introduction and management of change will be much easier and more successful. Because people act in accord with how they perceive things, the alignment and broadening of staff perceptions is essential to successfully implementing change.

Assess your situation and consider these actions :
- Inform yourself about the proposed changes - seek out facts from opinions. Discuss these with staff.
- Question the need for proposed changes.
- Make a list of the questions you would like answers to and ask your manager to discuss them with you.
- Consult with staff to be affected by the change before the change is announced.

- Consult with key stakeholders during the decision making stage.
- Discuss with and gain agreement from staff as to why change is necessary.
- Ask staff to discuss their perceptions and fears about the proposed changes with you.
- Discuss with staff the benefits and likely impact of the proposed changes.
- Demonstrate your support for the intended change.
- Ask informed outsiders to talk to staff about the new initiatives.
- Ask staff what they see as the likely obstacles to implementing the changes.
- Clarify the roles of yourself and staff once the change is implemented.
- Be honest when giving reasons for change.
- Establish the facts behind rumours and discuss these with staff.
- Discuss what needs to be done to implement the changes.
- Inform internal and external customers of the changes and the reasons behind them - where this is not counter-productive.
- Involve staff in developing an implementation strategy.
- Identify the specific actions which will need to be performed during implementation.
- Determine the priority of actions before implementation.
- Budget for the change to ensure adequate resourcing.
- Provide training or coaching in any new systems or procedures.
- Review the progress and impact of the change on a regular basis.

No passion so effectually robs the mind of all its
power of acting and reasoning as fear.

Edmund Burke, 1729-1797
English statesman, orator and writer
Letters on a Regicide Peace

Send reinforcements,
we're going to advance

Managers need to understand and apply the power of positive reinforcement in the process of managing the performance of their people. Getting staff to change their behaviour is one of the most difficult jobs for a manager. Although it is usually unintentional, many managers provide more negative reinforcement than positive reinforcement.

Here is some food for thought for managers on the subject of positive reinforcement:

- Once people start adopting a new behaviour, reinforcement by the manager will turn it into habit. It can take a lot of energy on the part of the manager to get staff to adopt a new way of doing things. But once started, a little regular reinforcement by the manager will help it to become the norm.

- Reinforce the new behaviour as soon as it becomes evident. Don't leave a long gap between the person trying the new ways of doing things and you applying the reinforcement. If a person experiences an immediate positive consequence from you they are more likely to repeat the behaviour.

- Look for opportunities to reinforce 'right efforts' as much as 'right results'. Improvement on past behaviours needs to be acknowledged and reinforced. Continue to reinforce results, but acknowledge that different people will move at their own pace. As long as there is positive movement, it should be reinforced. If you want people to achieve new standards, set goals for those standards and look to reinforce both the attainment of those standards and progress toward them.

- While people are learning and practising the new ways of doing things, keep the reinforcement continuous. Once they have adopted the new ways as standard practice and they do them all the time, reinforcement can be less frequent. As people experience the better consequences of the new ways of doing things, the reinforcers become inherent to the new behaviour. People will become more self-reinforcing.

- Very few job behaviours are mutually exclusive - the same behaviours are used over a wide range of job tasks. By reinforcing new behaviours in one aspect of a person's job performance, you will increase the application of those new behaviours (and the associated learnings for the individual) in other aspects of their job performance. The impact of reinforcement spreads into other areas of job performance.

- Positive reinforcement needs to be specific so that the person knows exactly what it is that they have improved. Saying to somebody, "You are doing a good job", is not as effective as telling them exactly what it is that you have observed. Ask people to tell you where they think they have improved.

- All people are different to degrees more or less, so you need to be aware that what is reinforcing to you may not be to another. Whatever you say or do by way of a reinforcement has to be perceived as a positive reinforcement by the person. Discuss what you have said or done, explain why and check for their reaction.

Once removed

 The chain is only as strong as its weakest link.
English proverb

How often does the person in the 'front line' have to apologise for delays, errors or misinformation caused by or provided by staff 'once removed' from direct customer contact? Do all your staff know the relationship between the quality of internal customer service and the quality of external customer service?

Many people in organisations work in isolation and ignorance as to where they fit into the big picture. They may also be unaware of how their work impacts on the work of others. As a manager it is essential that you ensure that all your staff know the consequences of their actions or inactions on other staff, in any given situation.

Should you want to improve the internal client relationships within your organisation or area these actions will provide a sound starting point.

- Discuss the concept of internal client-supplier relationships, the concept of client driven quality with staff and the need to provide superior value service.
- Identify ways we can exceed the expectations of our clients.
- Discuss the impact the organisation support services have on the delivery of services to your customers.
- Ask internal clients for their expectations and perceptions of the quality of service they are provided with and then incorporate these in your plans to improve things.
- Identify, define, document and discuss the main things you do which impact on

the delivery of services to internal clients.

- Discuss clients expectations/perceptions of services with all staff in your area.
- Check that you have the capability to meet your client's expectations for each of the key processes performed in your area.
- Establish and discuss standard procedures for all key processes.
- Discuss the importance of and the reasons why things are done the way they are and ask staff how each key process could be performed better.
- Identify what our clients need to do to help us help them.
- Identify non-value adding activities, i.e. those things which seem to be a waste of time. Involve staff in this process as it will help them to understand the reasons why things need to be done.
- Conduct reviews on a regular basis to monitor client perceptions of our services.
- Gain the support of senior management for your plans to improve your services and discuss what they need to do to help you make the changes.
- Implement changes to the way we do things so as to improve our services. This is important - we often identify the problem and then do nothing about it. You may wish to consider incorporating client suggestions, where appropriate, into the new ways of doing things.
- Provide feedback to staff regularly regarding client perceptions of our services. They need to know exactly what the perceptions of others are regardless of whether these perceptions are right or wrong. 'Self awareness is the beginning of all learning.'
- Check regularly that all key processes performed by your area are capable of meeting client expectations.
- Acknowledge the efforts of individual staff who make efforts to improve our services.
- Provide training, coaching and/or mentoring to staff who need assistance in providing improved client service.

Customer's last stand

Just as beauty is in the eye of the beholder, quality is in the eye of the user or customer. It doesn't really matter what we think about the quality of our products or services. What really matters is what our customers think.

Every work group has a number of internal customers to which they provide products or services. The performance of our team, by way of the quality of our products or services, affects the ability of our internal customers to supply high quality products or services to our external customers - the ones who justify our existence, create our profits and pay our salaries.

A manager needs to ensure that team members understand and accept that we exist to meet or exceed the expectations of both our external and internal customers. Most team members these days accept the focus on external customers, but they may not see that the focus on internal customers is also important.

As with our external customers, the team needs to know the expectations and perceptions of our internal customers about the quality of our service to them.

Opposite is a simple survey a manager can use with internal customers to improve the quality of the products or services provided to them. Arrange to send this customer survey to your internal customers and ask them to complete it in relation to your work group.

Once you have the assessment back from your internal customers, discuss the results with your team and agree ways to improve the quality of our products and services to each internal customer. Meet with your internal customers and discuss the implementation of ways to improve quality and any support you might require from them.

Internal Customer Service - quality assessment

	LOW				HIGH
	1	2	3	4	5
• The extent that we identify your needs and expectations.					
• The extent our products or services meet your needs.					
• The extent our products or services meet your expectations.					
• The extent that our systems, procedures and systems assist you.					
• The extent that our capability permits us to meet your needs.					
• The extent that we understand your problems and concerns.					
• The extent that we assist you to resolve your problems.					
• The extent that we seek feedback about the quality of our products or services.					
• The extent that we act on feedback.					
• The extent that we follow up to check that improvements have been made					

As a supplier of products and services to your work group, what would you like us to :

1. Do more of ...   3. Start doing ...

2. Do less of...   4. Change ...

to improve the quality of our service to you.

Stand and deliver

Isaac Newton's third law of motion - every action has an equal and opposite reaction - has some application in the dynamics of organisational performance. The performance of every individual is linked in some way to the overall performance of the organisation and the actions of each person impact either directly or indirectly on every other person. Everything that happens in an organisation is connected in some way. Nothing happens in isolation of some other happening. If it does, then it needs to be eliminated because it is a non-value adding activity.

In the internal customer-supplier relationships, a manager's work team will have a number of internal suppliers providing it with materials, processing, information, advice, decisions, procedures, systems, equipment, etc. For example, internal suppliers to a work team are human resources, information technology, stores, financial accounting and other departments. Their primary reason for existence is to provide a service to other parts of the organisation to assist the performance of work teams. Unfortunately, these internal suppliers don't always see it that way.

Opposite is a tool that a manager can use to improve the quality of services received from an internal supplier. In this case, the focus is on the human resources department but you can use this with any internal service provider.

Complete the assessment and the statements and discuss ways to improve the quality of their services with the human resources department.

Assessment of the Service Quality
of the Human Resources Department

	NO				YES
	1	2	3	4	5
• Informs us of the range of services they can provide.					
• Advises us of how they can assist our work group.					
• Provides prompt responses to questions, queries, requests.					
• Visits our location to identify our needs, circumstances and issues.					
• Provides accurate and up-to-date information.					
• Explains how we can incorporate human resource services into improving team performance.					
• Provides services related to our needs.					
• Identifies and meets our expectations.					
• Advises us of what assistance is available to assist us to deal with human resource issues on site.					
• Follows up to identify if there are any on-going problems after using their services.					
• Understands organisational blockages that adversely affect our team performance.					
• Understands management blockages that adversely affect our team performance.					
• Checks our satisfaction with the service provided.					
• Seeks our input on ways to improve the quality of their services.					

To assist our team performance, we would like you (the HR dept) to:

1. Do more of ...   3. Start doing ...

2. Do less of...   4. Change ...

Tell and show

During a half time break many years ago, the coach of an Australian Rules Football team was not happy with his players. He started to address them softly saying, "When I was a little boy.....my mother told me about some little things which had wings. They sparkled and flitted around from place to place leaving trails of star dust. (Pause) .....She told me they were called 'Fairies' (Another pause) ..... In my whole life I haven't seen one." Then suddenly at the top of his voice he screamed out, "....but today I've seen 18 of them....." The tirade went on.

In the past, many coaches used to scream and shout and abuse their players because it was considered to be the way that coaching was done. Think of the consequences the above scenario had on the players. What were the intelligent ones thinking during that 'fairy tale'?

Nowadays, with a greater awareness of what constitutes good coaching, we have come to realise that good coaching is about research, analysis, remediation, support, techniques and practise. Good coaches are caring, intelligent, fair and empathetic. They also know their pupil and treat them according to their levels of ability, development and individuality.

Managers will often need to coach or provide a coach for a staff member to help them achieve a higher standard. Here are some pointers to successful coaching.

- Provide a coach who is respected by the trainee.
- Use aids and practical situations to make the coaching session relevant.
- Look for opportunities to praise the 'trainee'.
- Use words the trainee understands.
- Be honest about your own skills and knowledge.
- Allow for discussion time when planning a coaching session.
- Act to reduce distractions during a coaching session.
- Ask the trainee for their knowledge about the area being covered.
- Organise yourself, the content and objectives and prepare for the session thoroughly prior to coaching.
- Explain the 'big picture' and the intended outcomes of the coaching sessions.
- Involve the trainee at all times during coaching sessions by encouraging two way communication.
- Be aware the coaching task is not complete until the objective has been achieved.
- Act on feedback about your coaching effectiveness immediately.
- Monitor results of coaching.
- Discuss the role of the coach.
- Set up the coaching session.
- Identify exactly what the person needs to learn. Tell the person what to do, how to do it and why it is important. Show them how to do it. Ask for questions or things to show again. Get them to practise while you watch. Ask the trainee to describe in their own words the critical aspects of this job, the key things to do and/or the critical safety issues. Ask the trainee what they would do differently if a mistake has occurred while they are practising a skill. Give feedback on what they did well and what needs improvement. Get them to practise again. Give feedback. And so on until the person can do it.
- Identify areas still requiring improvement and repeat the above coaching process.

In one ear and out the other

As a manager how good are you at communicating? Do you check to ensure the intended message was received? Because something is clear in your mind it may not be clear in the minds of others. We often take for granted that people see things the way we do. The fact is, they often don't.

The way we interpret things varies significantly from person to person. For whatever reason, when two people are reading the same text or listening to the same story they may be processing this information in different ways. As a result their understandings and responses will vary.

Workplace communication is about providing information to staff about something, and staff then demonstrating their understanding to the satisfaction of the person providing the information or sending the message.

In organisations, there are hundreds of reasons why communication suffers. We all like to know what is going on. Good communication improves job satisfaction, staff morale and productivity.

- Communicate to staff an unpopular decision honestly and forthrightly.
- Discuss sensitive issues in a tactful way by taking the staff member aside and away from the hearing of others. Behind closed doors in neutral territory is a good place.
- Think through the consequences of an issue and the impact it may have on staff before you announce what is going to happen.
- Explain your thoughts about complex issues and the rationale for your thinking. It is useful to explain why something is important to you and the organisation.
- Seek feedback on key issues by finding out from staff what they think and how they feel.
- Seek clarification from staff to confirm they understand what is required of them.
- Ask staff to identify the nature and frequency of their communication requirements.
- Use the most appropriate method to communicate to staff, e.g. where a personal matter needs to be discussed.
- Discuss the existing communication systems and procedures and for what purpose they are to be used.
- Inform staff of the most correct and appropriate means of communication.
- Explain what channels of communication staff may use.
- Ask staff to comply with organisation communication systems and procedures.
- Respond to communication from others where a response is appropriate and warranted.
- Inform staff of when you will respond if you can't provide them with the information straight away.
- Review the effectiveness of your communication skills by analysing how often your intended message is not acted upon.
- Seek feedback on the effectiveness of communication systems and procedures.
- Seek feedback about your own communication style.
- Consult with staff about decisions which will affect them before final decisions are made.

Curiosity killed the cat,
information brought it back

> The information most useful to me ...comes from quick,
> and often casual verbal exchanges. This usually reaches a manager
> much faster than anything written down. And usually the more timely
> the information is, the more valuable it is.
> **Andrew Grove**
> *Chief Executive Officer, Intel Corp, High Output Management.*

For your information, this is the information age. Be informed or perish. You, your team members, your manager and other internal customers of your team need information. This information needs to be sufficient, accurate, timely and relevant.

You can use the following 'Workplace Information Analysis' to check that your team has the information it requires to perform to its optimum level. In looking at your team's requirements for information, you will be asked to identify or assess:

- The **essential** (E) and **desirable** (D) information which your team members need to successfully perform all their jobs.
- The **frequency** of their information requirements - daily, weekly, monthly.
- The **format** by which that information is presented.
- **From whom** and **for whom** the information is required.
- The **sufficiency** of the information being provided from Low 1 2 3 4 5 High
- The **timeliness** of the information being provided from Poor 1 2 3 4 5 Good
- The **accuracy** of the information being provided from Low 1 2 3 4 5 High.

Do this analysis in consultation with your team to identify ways to improve the quantity and quality of information flow to your team. You can follow the same process to improve information flow from team members to you and between you and your manager.

Workplace Information Analysis - information requirements for staff

INFORMATION (what)	E/D	FREQUENCY			FORMAT	FROM WHOM	FOR WHOM	SUFF 1-5	TIME 1-5	ACC 1-5
		DLY	WKLY	MTLY						

"

An individual without information cannot
take responsibility; an individual who is given information
cannot help but take responsibility.

Jan Carlzon
Chief Executive Officer, SAS (Sweden),
Moments of Truth (Ballinger, 1987)

If you don't give people information, they'll make up
something to fill the void.

Carla O'Dell
President, O'Dell and Associates, CFO, October, 1987.

"

37

The mushroom syndrome

The 'mushroom syndrome' - keep them in the dark and feed them bull.... appears to be alive and flourishing. Talk to employees down the line and they still tell you that they get insufficient information about what's going on. It's often too little, too late, inaccurate or not at all.

Some managers argue that communicating some things to employees would be counter-productive. Maybe. But look at the impact on morale, trust, co-operation and performance when organisations deal dishonestly with unpleasant information.

Communication is the life-blood of an organisation. In the absence of effective communication, workers will form their own opinions about many of the issues which affect their motivation and work performance. Unfortunately, this usually results in rumours, half-truths, distortions, misinterpretations and a general lack of understanding.

The root cause of many workplace problems is the different perceptions held by the various stakeholders. The old sayings, "oh what a wicked web we weave when at first we practice to deceive" and "honesty is the best policy" are just as relevant in the workplace.

What to communicate? These are some of the things about which people want information:
- The purpose and strategy of the team or work group to which they belong.
- The hard and soft, key performance indicators which inform them about the progress and outcomes of their work group.
- How the outcomes of their work group impact on the 'big picture'.
- Why we do things the way we do at all levels within the organisation.
- What impact their work performance has on both internal and external customers.
- How other areas of the organisation use the services or information provided by our area.
- The reasons behind existing policies and procedures which appear to the

worker to be obsolete or unnecessary.

- The reasons behind changes to policies and procedures.
- What things they do well and what things they do poorly or not so well.
- What the future looks like for the organisation and for the individual.
- What management are doing about their problems.
- The reasons why management aren't doing anything about their problems.

- What action management has taken to implement suggestions to improve systems and procedures.
- The rationale behind management's rejection or lack of action regarding suggestions to improve things.
- What things are happening which could affect their job security.
- The rationale behind policy decisions.
- How the organisation as a whole is performing.
- What opportunities exist to develop new skills or to seek advancement.
- What help is available to assist them to deal with personal problems which invariably affect on the job performance.
- What internal and external customers think of the products or services they are supplying.
- By what criteria their work performance is being judged.
- What the manager is doing about problems identified within the work group.
- Future changes which are likely to affect how they do their work.

What we have here is a failure to communicate

> No talent in management is worth more than the
> ability to master facts - not just any facts, but the ones that provide
> the best answers. Mastery thus involves knowing what facts you want;
> where to dig for them; how to dig; how to process the mined ore;
> and how to use the precious nuggets of information that are
> finally in your hand. The process can be laborious - which is why it is
> so often botched.
>
> **Robert Heller**
> *Editor, Management Today.*

The dominant cause of most organisations' internal problems is a breakdown in communications. The most important skill a manager can develop (with the possible exception of political savvy) is the art of communication. As subsets of the larger organisation, teams or work groups thrive on a constant diet of good communications.

- Identify the nature, the format and the timing of the communication requirements of the team.
- Ask where, when, how, what, why and with whom communication is breaking down.
- Identify individual requirements for information.
- Consult with other teams to agree your and their communication requirements and implement and monitor actions to achieve them.
- Ask team members for ways to improve communication within the team and with other teams.
- Hold regular communication sessions to allow two-way feedback on any issues important to the team.
- Ask staff to tell you what issues they want more information about.

- Discuss issues or changes with the team as soon as you are aware of them.
- Agree with the next level of management the communication requirements of your team.
- Provide (at least) monthly updates on team and organisation performance.
- Identify existing policies and procedures which cause poor communications.
- Seek clarification from team members to check their level of understanding.
- After team discussions always document what actions, by whom, by when, etc. will happen as a result of the discussion.
- In discussions with team members, separate facts from opinions. Ask people if what they say is based on fact or assumption.
- As rumours become known to you, discuss the facts behind the rumour within the team.
- Seek information from higher management on anything unclear to you and the team.
- Consult with team members about decisions which will affect them before the decision is made.
- When unpopular directives have to be communicated to the team, explain the rationale as best you can, your position, your feelings about the directive and let the team members express their feelings.
- In meetings, use visual aids to stress the important messages you are trying to convey.
- Regularly review how well we communicate as a team.
- Ask what you could do more of or less of to improve communications within the team and with other parts of the organisation.

START A RUMOUR THAT THERE'S A COMMUNICATION MEETING NEXT WEEK...

CHIEF

Read my lips

Is communicating with people a dying art form? Many people, invariably older than younger, appear to hold this view. And they can argue a case too. The impact of countless hours watching mind numbing television, the reduced need for face to face contact as computers, electronic mail and other technology relentlessly changes our work lives are some of the arguments.

Whatever you believe, there is no doubt that a manager with poor communication skills is severely handicapped when it comes to leading, inspiring and managing people.

Some people are better at communicating than others. Why is that so? What do they do or say which makes them stand out as skilled communicators? Why do people pay them more attention when they talk and act on what they say?

These are some of the things the better communicators do. They:

- Adopt a perspective which looks at the whole situation not just the parts of most interest to them.
- Declare if what they are expressing is fact or based on assumption or inference.
- Stay attendant and focused on you while you are talking.

- Allow you to finish your point without interrupting unless you're rambling.
- Show that they have been listening to you by commenting on what you have been saying.
- Pick up on a point which you have made and then expand on it further.
- Combine logic with passion and energy.
- Choose their words carefully and with precision so that what they say is what they mean to say. Avoid over-reactions, exaggerations and generalisations.
- Acknowledge points you have made which they agree with and ask you to elaborate on points on which they are unclear.
- Describe things as they perceive them to be without making any judgement about them.
- Use words which are simple to understand and in common usage.
- Start a conversation with a background statement to give you a context.
- Check your knowledge of the topic or situation instead of assuming that you know.
- Use anecdotes, imagery and their own experiences to create word pictures.
- Relate what they are saying to your situation or experiences.
- Speak up about their rights while at the same time acknowledging your rights in the situation.
- Watch your body language to see if you become disinterested or distracted.
- Stop talking when they see that you are distracted or have stopped listening. (Why would anyone keep talking when it's obvious that the other person is not listening?)
- Seek your opinion about things that they have said.
- Frequently check to see that they are being understood by asking you for your interpretation of the points they have been making.
- Describe the situation to you from your point of view.
- Express their ideas even when they differ from those around them and not get upset when someone disagrees with them.
- Describe the positive aspects of things rather than the negative aspects.

Rudyard Kipling's six wise men

One rhyme I learned during my student days which I have recalled many a time is:

Rudyard Kipling's six wise men
Who, what, where, how, why and when.

These 'six wise men' provide a simple, but very useful framework when analysing problems, writing brief reports or asking questions to obtain information about a situation. The 'information age' is well and truly upon us and managers are required to manage a vast amount of information. In fact, the quality and quantity of the information flowing to a manager is a key determinant in their effectiveness.

Not all of this information will be accurate, sufficient, reliable or timely which means the manager has to develop investigative skills - she needs to be able to ask the right questions in the right way at the right time.

Here are some points to consider in relation to the art of questioning :

- Identify clearly what you want to achieve by your questions.
- When the situation requires it, prepare a list of questions. Use a variety of questions even on the same theme. A question which elicits a 'don't know' answer could provide vital information when asked in a different way.
- Use 'closed' questions when seeking to confirm facts about the situation which are known to you or which you suspect. These are usually answered by 'yes' or 'no', e.g. "Did you kill that man?"
- Be aware that closed questions are of limited value. They can lead to this situation - "Why didn't you tell me that before?" "You didn't ask me."
- Use 'open' questions when you want to establish the facts about a situation or to broaden your lines of inquiry, e.g. "How did you kill that man?"
- Ask open questions which begin with the words - who, what, where, how, why and when.
- Avoid 'leading questions' which suggest the obvious answer. They may not elicit an honest response. They show your viewpoint and may cause others

to simply reflect your view, e.g. "I think I'm managing quite well, don't you?"

- If you are not satisfied with a person's response, ask the question again in another way.
- Be aware that some people in some circumstances will only tell you what they think you want to hear. Explain to people why you need the facts be they pleasant or unpleasant.
- Convince people that there will be no repercussions for telling the truth.
- Use questions which are direct and honest. Trick questions will create hostility and possibly provide misleading information.
- Use words that the person can understand and relate to - listen to their answer to see if they understood your question in the first place.
- Ask people to clarify whether what they are saying is based on fact or assumption or inference.
- When people respond to your questions with exaggerations ask them for specific details. "Look, this happens all the time." "All the time? What, daily?" "Well...no." "Weekly?" "No." "Monthly?" "No." "So when exactly did it last happen?" "Um...about three months ago."
- Check your own understanding of the answers you receive. If you are not absolutely clear, ask more questions.

Squeaky wheels need oiling (or replacing)

Complaints are rarely made without some foundation. Admittedly, some people complain more than others and some have great difficulty finding something positive to say about anything. There is also an element of mischief about the way some people in organisations 'raise issues'. Is there a political motive? What do they have to gain from this course of action? Is it a throwback to their childhood and an adult form of 'attention seeking behaviour'?

Complaints can be time consuming for the manager if they are to get to the bottom of the problem. However, they can be more time consuming if they are not dealt with and resolved quickly.

Managing complaints in a way that is fair and equitable is no mean feat. More to the point though, what are the main things about which people complain? If we know what they are, maybe we can ensure we are not guilty of giving then grounds to complain in the first place.

People complain about:

- Being overworked.
- Being underworked.
- Lack of communication.
- Unsafe workplaces or practices.
- Lack of co-operation from other areas.
- Poor work conditions.

- Physical and mental intimidation.
- Unfair treatment for themselves or others.
- Not enough pay.
- Errors affecting them or their work.
- Other people not doing the right thing.
- People not listening to them.
- Not having a chance to have their say.
- Angry or rude customers.
- Being poorly managed.
- Poor policy.
- Lack of role clarification.
- Perceived indifference to their problems from management.
- Management failure to make hard decisions.
- Lack of direction from management.
- Boring work.
- Favouritism.
- Not knowing what the goals of the organisation are.
- Others not doing their bit.
- Managers not having the experience.
- Advertising campaigns that raise unrealistic customer expectations.
- Lack of acknowledgment for doing a good job.
- Apparently irrational change.
- No overtime.
- No lunch breaks / rest time.
- Having to do more with less.
- Unrealistic / unfair sales targets.
- No career opportunities.
- Restructuring.
- Sexism.
- Sexual harassment.
- Faulty or obsolete equipment.

Lose the battle - win the war

> The aim of argument, or of discussion,
> should not be victory, but progress.
> **Joseph Joubert**
> *Pensees (1842), 7.31, tr. Katharine Lyttelton.*
>
> When we wish to correct with advantage, and to show another
> that he errs, we must notice from what side he views the matter,
> for on that side it is usually true.
> **Pascal**
> *Pensees (1670), 9, tr. W.F. Trotter*
>
> The partisan, when he is engaged in a dispute, cares nothing
> about the rights of the question, but is anxious only to convince his
> hearer of his own assertions.
> **Socrates**
> *in Plato's Phaedo (4th - 3rd c. B.C.), tr. Benjamin Jowett*

When groups of people are together for a period of time, it is inevitable that there will be clashes. How we deal with personality clashes is all important for the maintenance of harmony, motivation and productivity.

It helps to realise and accept that because someone doesn't do things the way we would like them done or doesn't agree with our point of view, doesn't necessarily mean that they are wrong. We draw on the ability to make decisions and form opinions from all the factors which shape our lives. Background, upbringing, socio-economic environment, culture, age, gender, religion, experiences, education, opportunity, luck, etc. all influence how we think. These factors influence how we perceive things and we respond and act according to our perceptions.

- Consider the merits of opinions which differ from yours by actually listing the points which are valid, correct or beneficial to the issue in question.
- Demonstrate respect for an opposing point of view by allowing it to be expressed and actively listening to what is being said.
- Discuss the for and against for both points of view.
- Seek assistance from colleagues to act as mediators in situations where it is you in conflict with someone else.
- Consider the interests of, and consequences on, all stakeholders when decisions are made.
- Adopt a compromise position when both parties hold strongly opposing viewpoints and where the end result is not crucial. Never compromise safety.
- Change your position when you are presented with facts unknown to you.
- Describe a conflict situation from the other person's point of view.
- Check to see that the other party is satisfied after a resolution has been reached. "Speak now or forever hold your peace."
- Identify the rights, needs and interests of all parties in a conflict situation.
- Ask for and receive feedback about your own style or manner. This can be done by asking your own peers or staff what you should do less of or more of in relation to conflict resolution.
- Ask yourself "what are the consequences if I concede the point?"
- Concede ground when to win the point would cause more trouble than it's worth.
- Avoid saying things which may damage the dignity and self-respect of others. Focus only on the point of disagreement not the person.
- Stop the conversation and suggest another time to continue when tempers 'flare'.
- Agree 'early in the piece' that you will act to resolve any points of disagreement.
- Agree that an issue is finished once a decision is made.
- Avoid 'clouding' work issues with unassociated problems.
- Seek professional advice where you find you are in conflict with many people about many issues. It may be you who is the problem.
- Hold discussions when your mind is fresh and clear - when you are more likely to be reasonable.

Winning isn't everything

Anytime you have two or more people together in the workplace, you have potential for conflict. A large chunk of a manager's time is spent dealing with conflict. Conflict does not have to be associated with anger, violence or even ill feeling.

Conflict can occur any time there is a difference of interests, understanding, values or beliefs, style, opinions or perceptions. The consequences of conflict can be anger, sadness, frustration, stress, disappointment, violence, waste, confusion, etc.

It is generally accepted that there are five ways of dealing with conflict. There is no single 'best' way - the situation and the consequences of how the conflict is addressed will indicate the best approach for each situation.

DO NOTHING when:
- An issue is trivial or there is something else to do which is more important.
- You have absolutely no chance of winning.

- Winning the point will cause more trouble than its worth.
- Tempers need to calm down to allow a clear perspective.
- Someone else can handle the situation better.
- You need to gather facts about the situation.
- You need to clarify your own thoughts about the situation.

DOMINATE when :
- An emergency calls for quick, decisive action.
- Non-negotiable points have to be enforced.

CONCEDE when :
- You are in the wrong and you need to be seen to be reasonable.
- The issue is more important to others than it is to you.
- You need someone to do something for you.
- You need to cut your losses if you are losing and your situation will not get better.
- You need to gain favours for another time.
- The relationship is more important than you being right.

COMPROMISE when :
- You need a temporary settlement to a complicated issue.
- Time is running out and you need a workable solution.
- You are up against an equal with an opposite goal.
- Your point is important but not worth the time and hassle of being more assertive.
- Your personal goals and the relationship are both of moderate importance.

COLLABORATE when :
- Each person's position is too important to compromise and the relationship is important.
- You need to learn something from others.
- You need to unify different points of view.
- You need to get total commitment from all.
- It is important to repair a damaged relationship.

Two heads are better than one

> ❝
> A man who listens because he has nothing to say
> can hardly be a source of inspiration. The only listening that counts is
> that of the talker who alternately absorbs and expresses ideas.
> **Agnes Repplier**
> *'The Luxury of Conversation,' Compromises (1904)*
> ❞

As we move into the 21st century, the people we manage and with whom we work will, on average, be getting older. With age comes experience and with experience, knowledge. In many organisations, we have an untapped workforce in terms of helping set the course and steer the ship.

During any decision making process, the combined knowledge of the group will usually exceed the sum of the knowledge of the individuals making up the group. Planning together has some huge benefits for all involved in the process. The learning gained and the commitment to the decision are but two of them.

Consultation is about giving and receiving, sharing, listening, discussing and making decisions together. We can tap into the well of knowledge which too often sits wasted in organisations - our workforce!

- Discuss and agree the purpose and intended outcomes of a consultative planning process.
- Determine which staff will form the consultative planning team.
- Agree a team co-ordinator - someone who will arrange meetings, set agendas, follow up on decisions made and manage the 'housekeeping' for the group.
- Discuss with staff the benefits of consultative planning.

- Identify and agree the key areas around which consultative planning will happen.
- Identify and agree the role and responsibilities of team members and the co-ordinator.
- Identify all stakeholders to be affected by the outcomes of the planning process.
- Identify the nature of the input required from all stakeholders.
- Obtain facts, opinions and perceptions from all stakeholders.
- Incorporate these facts, opinions and perceptions in the planning process.
- Establish and document a schedule, the frequency and venue of meetings.
- Discuss, identify and use the strengths and experience of all team members.
- Discuss and identify the needs of staff in relation to the planning process and the strategic direction of the organisation.
- Seek information from others who are already successfully using consultative planning.
- Observe other planning teams in action.
- Prepare an agenda for planning meetings.
- Discuss and agree the roles of staff in the consultative process.
- Discuss and agree the strategies and resources to be used during implementation.
- Discuss with and inform customers about what consultative planning is and how they and staff will benefit.
- Review the progress of the planning process regularly.
- Discuss ways to improve the planning process once a review has been undertaken.
- Discuss with senior management what they need to do to support the consultative planning process.
- Report back to management about your results.

We've always done it this way

To improve is to change;
to be perfect is to change often.
Winston Churchill, 1874-1965
English Prime Minister, writer and soldier

Decay is inherent in all compounded things. Strive on with diligence.
Buddha (Prince Siddhartha), 563?-483? B.C.
Indian philosopher and founder of Buddhism

The great man is the man who does a thing for the first time.
Alexander Smith, 1830-1867
Scottish poet

Fortunately, one of the driving forces of the human race is the desire to improve; to do things new, different and better than we do them today. And thus slowly we evolve as a species. There will always be a better way.

The culture of an organisation - the way we do things - is dictated by established policies, systems and procedures. Who are best placed to spot the flaws in systems and procedures? The people who apply them in the workplace and who are closest to the customer - be they external or internal.

Never take for granted that because "this is how we have always done it" it is the best way. There are many ways to get the same result - some ways are certainly more efficient than others.

Most staff, when confronted by a procedure which through experience they know to be inefficient, obsolete or downright stupid, will invent better ways of doing things.

Involve your work group or team in finding those better ways.

- Identify, define and document the key procedures used by our team.
- Define and agree the purpose for all key procedures.
- Discuss standard procedures and their purpose with staff.
- Identify where systems and procedures are not being followed.
- Determine the reasons they are not being followed.
- Identify the causes of inefficient systems and procedures.
- Identify things we do which seem to be a waste of time
- Make sure staff are aware of how the outcomes of our systems and procedures benefit other parts of the organisation or our customers.
- Ask staff to suggest better ways of doing things.
- Ask the beneficiaries or customers of our procedures if they can suggest better ways of doing things.
- Discuss with staff the consequences of their suggestions on all internal and external customers.
- Discuss with your manager and peers the actions and support you require from them to improve systems and procedures.
- Discuss with staff how to implement agreed changes to systems and procedures.
- Implement agreed changes to existing procedures or new procedures and monitor the application and results of the new ways of doing things.
- Inform internal and external customers of the changes and the reasons behind them.
- Recognise and acknowledge the efforts of staff who act to develop new, different and better ways of doing things.
- Provide on-going training and coaching to staff in following and implementing systems and procedures.
- Encourage staff informally to always look for better ways of doing things.
- Every 6 months hold a meeting to formally review the ways we do things and to identify better ways of doing things.

Remember, small improvements can make a big difference.

What do they really think?

> The dogs bark, but the caravan moves on.
> **Arabic proverb**

How an organisation is perceived by staff can really affect the quality of product and service provided by them and in turn the level of business and sales generated.

It would be nice to think that all staff possess the 'corporate loyalty' which helps organisations become profitable and successful. Unfortunately this is not the case. In many organisations there is often underlying resentment of management and, in many cases, open resentment of management and the organisation for which they work.

Cost cutting and job losses have left many employees resentful and bitter. The cry from governments and business for higher productivity and cost reduction have resulted in these employees working longer hours, being laid off through redundancies (if they're lucky) or sackings (if they're not), lower pay or more work for the same pay. Whatever the case, there is a need to repair some of the damage that has been caused. The problem for managers is how can they change the perceptions of staff about the organisation, from the negative to the positive. Bear in mind this is not about having a 'warm and fluffy' workplace where every one is happy. It is about creating an environment in which staff value the work that they do and want to do the right thing by the organisation. The end result being greater productivity and thus greater profits and higher return for shareholders.

- Decide that you will make a conscious decision to establish positive perceptions about the organisation and set up a working group representative of a cross - section of staff to be involved in the exercise.

- Discuss the concept of perceptions and the differences between fact, inference and opinion, and symptom and cause.
- Discuss the concept of corporate loyalty, why it is important and the desired image of how we want to be seen in the marketplace.
- Discuss the impact both negative and positive perceptions have on the day to day operations of the organisation, i.e. staff motivation, morale, productivity and performance.
- Survey staff as to their perceptions of the organisation. This can be done by using outside expertise to conduct organisational climate surveys. Or design and develop your own staff perceptions survey. If you choose to do it yourself then consult with staff as to the content and design of the survey. Identify key areas about which staff form perceptions.
- Ask staff why they hold the perceptions they do of the organisation. Do this in a non - threatening environment and where open discussion can take place.
- Discuss with staff what would need to be done to change any negative perceptions. They will have ideas which are often sensible and effective.
- Ask staff what they can do to change any negative perceptions they may hold.
- Assess the accuracy of perceptions by discussing them with staff and management. Where there is uncertainty about the accuracy of perceptions, providing verifiable examples will clarify the 'truth'.
- Identify areas of communication breakdown that result in poor perceptions and discuss possible reasons for these perceptions.
- Explain the impact the 'big picture' has on management policies which appear unfair.
- Celebrate the organisation's wins by rewarding staff, e.g. paying the often promised bonus, providing morning tea, personally thanking staff.
- Identify ways to share the positive perceptions held by staff and what is required to be a 'good' corporate citizen.
- Form an organisation social committee and encourage staff to participate. Sponsor this group and let it be known this has been done.
- Reward and recognise staff who promote the organisation in a positive light.
- Discuss with senior management the support required from them to develop positive staff perceptions.

Count every cent - every cent counts

Get wealth when you have it not;
guard what you have got;
increase what you have guarded;
and bestow on worthy persons what you have increased.
Panchatantra
(c. 5th c.) 1, Franklin Egerton

With money in your pocket, you are wise and you are
handsome and you sing well too.
Yiddish Proverbs
(1949), ed. Hanan J. Ayalti

In today's increasingly competitive environment, there is constant pressure to reduce costs. The organisational budget is not a bottomless pit which can throw money at everything people want. Responsible cost management must exist. Managers themselves can't do it alone - they need the assistance of their staff.

The trick to reducing costs, without pain, lies in gaining agreement from all stakeholders that there is firstly, a need to do so and secondly, a willingness to take action to reduce costs.

Part of this process is through consultation with, and the education of, these stakeholders.

- Discuss and agree with all stakeholders the need to reduce costs.
- Discuss the benefits of reducing costs to the organisation and individuals.

- Brainstorm ideas with staff about ways in which costs can be reduced.
- Identify and discuss major overhead costs and areas where excessive costs are evident.
- Explain to staff why cost reduction in an identified area is important and what the consequences are if costs are not reduced.
- Establish a strategy to reduce costs and inform all staff of this strategy. Involve staff in developing the strategy.
- Begin implementing ways to reduce costs.
- Ensure that cost reductions will not result in adverse consequences to staff, customers or the organisation.
- Inform customers of your intentions to reduce costs in the identified area and the reasons why this is happening. If the cost reduction is going to affect customer service, apologise for this.
- Provide feedback about cost savings to staff and customers.
- Allocate cost savings to other areas where there is identified need for extra funding.
- Inform staff where the saved money will now be spent, i.e. other areas, debt reduction, capital purchases or new equipment.
- Set targets as to anticipated and expected cost reductions and discuss these with staff.
- Monitor progress and provide feedback to staff about how the targets are going and what efforts have resulted in the most effective reductions.
- Recognise and reward staff who make a concerted effort to reduce costs.
- Check that cost reductions do not adversely affect the day to day operations of the organisation by seeking feedback from staff in these areas.

Choices and consequences

> When a man asks your advice,
> he usually tells you just how he expects you to decide.
> **Edgar Watson Howe**
> *Country Town Sayings (1911)*
>
> We may give advice but we cannot inspire conduct.
> **La Rouchefoucauld**
> *Maxims (1665)*
>
> A hundred sage counsels are lost upon one who cannot take advice;
> a hundred bits of wisdom are lost upon the unintelligent.
> **Panchatantra**
> *(c. 5th c.), 1, tr. Franklin Edgerton*

Counselling is about identifying the cause of problems and agreeing how to address the cause. Sometimes a staff member has personal problems which may affect their work and their health. More often than not we assume the role of counsellor by virtue of our position as the person's manager. In many cases, it is not within our sphere of influence to solve the problem, but at least we can provide a starting point.

Providing advice through telling a person to do or not to do something doesn't always have the required effect. To solve the problem will require a sustained effort. To get a sustainable positive solution takes more than many of us are able or willing to do. Having said all that, there are some things which we can say and do which will make the counselling process easier.

• Speak to staff members in private away from their peers and in most circumstances without their peers knowing.

- Encourage the staff members to discuss their problems with you by providing a forum specific to discussing these sorts of issues.
- Encourage the staff member being counselled to start the conversation.
- Ask them where they see the root of the problem to be.
- Listen actively to what they are saying by paraphrasing their main points.
- Avoid making value judgements, i.e. avoid saying whether things are good or bad, right or wrong.
- Refrain from apportioning blame to the cause of the problem.
- Focus on the offending behaviours and not the person. Do this by saying things like "when you lose your temper it is unsettling to the others in the office." rather than "You are unsettling to others in the office when you lose your temper." Explain the consequences of any behaviour in question - explain how it affects others, staff morale, productivity, customers perceptions about the organisation and interpersonal relationships.
- Offer to provide professional advice where you may not be able to help.
- Avoid taking sides where a problem involves more than one party.
- Separate fact from assumption.
- Ask people for their opinions, what they think and feel about the situation.
- Ask the staff member for their consent to document issues of a sensitive nature if you feel further action needs to be taken by someone other than yourself.
- Assure the staff member that the discussions you are holding are confidential if you are not going to tell anyone else.
- Avoid discussing confidential matters with others - use a hypothetical situation if you are seeking answers to a problem.
- Ask the staff member for their consent to inform others should you feel it to be necessary.
- Treat all problems as important regardless of your impressions.
- Provide an opportunity for the staff member to calm down should they be upset.
- Encourage staff members to solve their own problems.
- Brainstorm solutions.
- Ensure your body language is supportive of their feelings.
- Hold discussions in a neutral environment.
- Provide undivided attention during the counselling session.

Switch off and switch on

When the performance of a good worker deteriorates for no apparent reason, there is a good chance that the employee has a personal problem weighing heavily on their mind. There are many factors which affect a person's job performance, but off-the-job problems are more often the cause of poor work performance than many managers realise.

These are problems related to some event occurring in their personal life such as death or illness in the family, divorce or the break-up of a relationship, problems with their children, financial difficulties, etc. What a person does in their private life is of course their concern, but if it starts to affect their performance at work, it becomes the manager's concern. Some action is required on the part of the manager, but this needs to be handled carefully and with sensitivity.

Your major purpose is not to provide a solution - it is highly unlikely that you can. Your main aim is to let the person know that she or he can talk to you about it if they want to and that you will listen and act as a sounding board. As professional counsellors will tell you, just letting a person 'get it off their chest' helps them feel much better about their problem. Time to put on your 'counsellor' hat.

- Be wary of imposing your solution on their problem - be prepared to do more listening than talking. Demonstrate that you really are listening by paraphrasing things they say and acknowledging how they might be feeling and how you would feel in the same circumstances.
- Begin by acknowledging their previous good performance.
- Let them know that you value them as a person and as a worker.
- Tell them that you have noticed a change in their behaviour. Describe the specific changes.
- Describe how you see these changes affecting their work and the work of others.
- Ask them how they feel they are currently handling their job. Reach agreement on your view and their view of their job performance.
- Check if there are any problems at work which are affecting them.

- Tell them that their private life is their business, but when it starts to affect their work it has to become your business.
- Assure them that anything you discuss will be kept strictly confidential and that no record of this conversation will be kept.
- Re-assure them that every one of us has personal problems which affect us at some time or other. If possible, cite an example of something which you had to deal with which really got you down.

- Encourage them to open up and discuss what it is that is distracting them.
- Ask them if they need some time off to deal with the problem.
- Ask them if they need help in dealing with their problem.
- Ask them if they would like to 'brainstorm' some actions they could take to help resolve their problem.
- Help them develop an action plan.
- Let them know that you will be supportive and that you can make allowances, but that their job performance needs to return to normal.
- Suggest appropriate professional counselling such as Lifeline.
- Suggest that you meet again in a week's time to see how things are.
- Invite them to talk to you about it at any time.

You can do better than that

Using agreed indicators of performance, managers can monitor the efforts and outcomes of both team and individual performance. When team and/or individual performance don't come up to the required standards, it's the manager's responsibility to take corrective action.

In the case of individuals, the manager needs to act in such a way as to convince the individual to improve and to do it without resistance. The consequences of doing nothing when a member of the work group is not performing can be serious.

It will frustrate other members of the team and affect your credibility as a manager as well as affect external and internal customers of your work group. It is important that you are seen to act to address the situation by other members of your team.

You can try and force compliance through threats and penalties, but for these to work you will probably have to apply them continuously and you are unlikely to change the root cause of the problem. You can get somebody to do something against their will, but they are likely to do it half-heartedly, or make it a low priority, or do it at a sub-standard level or find some way to sabotage your efforts.

Your goal is to have the person willing to change their behaviour. Try these guidelines to improving performance:

- Prior to the meeting, collect behavioural evidence related to the problem.
- Set up a meeting in private.
- Explain that you have a problem and that you need their help to resolve it.
- Set the condition that each person talks without interruption until they have finished their point.
- State what you perceive to be the situation. Describe things objectively without making any judgement.
- Explain the consequences of the situation on you, other members of the team and on other stakeholders including the person themself.
- Explain why it is important that you have to do something and why you are having this discussion. Explain that the only way to really resolve the situation is with their co-operation.
- Ask them how they view the situation. How they rate their performance. How they compare with others.
- Ask them what's causing the situation. Are there things happening that you are unaware of? Are they not happy working here? Discuss what you see as causing the situation.
- Ask them how their current behaviour is benefiting them.
- Discuss solutions together. Add your own suggestions when no worthwhile suggestions are raised or you want to extend those given.
- Agree what action each of you will take to resolve the situation. Both parties should note the same agreements.
- Agree a time frame for when you expect performance to be satisfactory.
- Agree a date and time to meet again and review the situation.
- Discuss the choices that each of you can make in this situation. Ask them to consider the probable consequences if the situation continues for both of you including consequences for non-compliance.
- Ask if they feel that you have treated them fairly. Let them know that you believe that they are capable of better and that is what you expect of them.
- Tell them that you will keep reviewing the situation with them until it is resolved.

The world is your oyster

I t's a competitive jungle out there - you have to strive to survive. In a
football game, the more times you present yourself at the ball, the more
likely you are to win the ball. The same philosophy applies in sales. The
more times you present yourself in the market place, the more chance you
have of attracting sales.

If you manage a sales team, here are a number of ways you and your team can
create business opportunities.

- Develop a list of potential 'referral giving' clients - these are clients who are
  pleased with our services and would be happy to recommend us to colleagues,
  associates, family or friends.
- Ask for referrals while visiting clients' premises.
- Ask for referrals at the end of a satisfactory business transaction.
- Call existing customers to promote other products which will benefit them.
- Review directories and registries of businesses (Dunn and Bradstreet,
  Business Who's Who, etc.) at the local library to obtain prospective customers.
- Read the business section of the daily newspapers.
- Check what's happening in the community newspapers.
- Obtain a list of the members of chambers of commerce.
- Research the background of target businesses/organisations.
- Develop and send letters of introduction incorporating benefit statements.
- Make follow up telephone calls within one day of receipt of the letter.
- Contact other people in your own organisation for sales referrals.
- Check that the person you are dealing with has the authority to make a buying
  decision.
- Drive around business/industrial areas to identify potential customers.
- Join business clubs and associations.
- Contact old connections from previous roles/employment.
- Segment our existing client base by product usage, volume and sales.
- Contact local government bodies for information on new business
  developments.
- Contact existing customers to check that everything is okay and if they have any

needs you can assist them with.
- Develop 'rainmaker' contacts in the marketplace. These are people who can refer business to you.
- Contact existing customers when a new product is launched to promote the new product.
- Offer to demonstrate new products or product innovations to existing customers and to business associations/clubs.
- Provide special rewards for key customers.

CREATING NEW BUSINESS..

Can't see the wood for the trees

CAN'T SEE THE WOOD FOR THE TREES...

From our early days at school right through to higher education, we are trained to be rational, logical, analytical and judgmental in our thinking process. While this type of thinking clearly has its place, it can stifle our ability to be creative and blind us to other ways of thinking and doing.

Most managers are guilty to some degree of attempting to apply routine or traditional solutions to new problems. It is easy to fall into a mental rut and miss seeing opportunities to be creative or innovative. If the nature of the problem is unchanged, then resolve it in the same way that has been successful in the past. The trouble is that few things stay the same - the nature of most things is constantly changing.

Here are some ways to break out of routine and habit when it comes to thinking. A manager can use these alone or with their staff in resolving problems or in developing innovative products, services or strategies.

FANTASY
- Clearly define the problem or opportunity.
- Assume that anything goes. Ignore all normal constraints and limitations.
- Fantasise with statements such as :
  - What I really need to do is....
  - What really needs to happen is....
  - The only way I can solve this problem would be if....
- Now make realistic statements such as :
  - Although I cannot really do that, I can....
  - It might be possible to do that, but first I would have to....

HYPOTHETICAL
- Clearly define the problem or opportunity.
- Develop a series of hypothetical statements related to the problem. What would happen if....? Ignore 'what is' about the situation and focus on creating hypothetical situations which don't currently exist. Don't evaluate the statements as you think of them. Go for quantity no matter how ridiculous your thoughts may be.
- Now use these statements to stimulate your thinking about what may be possible.

ASSOCIATION
- Write the problem on a whiteboard.
- Show a large picture unrelated to the problem to a group. Ask them to write down whatever words come to mind. All words or phrases are acceptable.
- Write a composite list of all these words and phrases on to the whiteboard.
- Taking each word or phrase separately, ask the group to try to associate the word with the problem to see whether this gives them any new ideas or solutions.

Standin' on the outside... lookin' in

Remember the term 'Jap crap'. It was a derogatory comment about the quality of the cheap Japanese products that started to flood the world market in the 50's and 60's. The general perceptions held by consumers was that all Japanese goods were of low quality. This was an image which took a long time to shake off.

Just what did Japanese management do to develop positive perceptions of Japanese products? The sorts of things they did took time to implement and years to bring about the desired change. Where your image is not tarnished the task will not be as difficult, but will require long term vision to achieve.

- Inform customers about the quality standards that are expected of your organisation during the provision of service or during production.
- Display the quality policy, vision and mission statements where customers will see them.
- Inform customers of the ethos and values of the organisation.
- Establish a company logo so that the customer associates your brand with high quality.
- Offer guarantees on quality of product.
- Train all staff in the need for 100% adherence to quality standards.
- Inform consumers of inspection processes and procedures that are undertaken to ensure quality.
- Acquire testimonial statements from influential people and authorities advocating the quality of our products and services. Inform customers of these.
- Establish, document and implement systems and procedures which exceed the minimum requirements of the industry standards.
- Train all representatives of the organisation in how to promote your products and services with quality as the key feature.
- Conduct tours of the organisation to demonstrate quality standards and to build a bond between the people who visit and the organisation.
- Change the name of products which consumers associate with poor quality or outdated products.
- Discuss with staff what they can do to promote the image of the organisation.

- Recognise and reward staff who actively promote the organisation in a positive way.
- Reward loyal customers with special privileges or gifts.
- Sponsor local community initiatives, e.g. sporting competitions, buildings, events, schools, charities.
- Satisfy customer complaints to the point where the customer's expectations of your response are far exceeded.
- Check that customers are happy with the product or service provided and act when the response is one of dissatisfaction.
- Ask customers what they believe your organisation can do to improve and where possible incorporate their suggestions in your improvement plan.
- Provide a money back guarantee on faulty product and inform the customer of any warranty agreements that may exist.
- Never make promises that staff in your organisation can't keep. Inform staff of the importance of not creating false expectations in the minds of customers.
- Train staff in providing exceptional customer service.

Opportunity only knocks once

Customers have two choices when they are dissatisfied. They can complain or just disappear never to be seen again. Many of them do the latter because the 'cost' of complaining is too high and they figure it is not worth the effort.

If customers are dissatisfied with the product or service, they are more likely to complain if they perceive your organisation as one that values complaints as opportunities to fix something. You need to show them that you are open and approachable and welcome their complaint as an opportunity to retain their business.

Below is a checklist a manager can use with staff in relation to reducing customer complaints or improving the way we respond to customer complaints.

- Inform customers of unexpected costs.
- Check to see that the product or service provided met their expectations.
- Ask customers for their perceptions of the products and services we provide.
- Ask customers for ways to improve our products and services.
- Incorporate customer suggestions into new ways of doing things.
- Make a note of all promises to customers and do what you say you will - always. Avoid creating expectations that can't be met.
- Provide accurate information at all times. If you don't know, find out the facts from someone who does.
- Use a problem solving approach such as, "Thank you for bringing this to my attention. It is very annoying when things like this happen. I'll look into this immediately and get back to you."
- Identify the exact cause of the customer's complaint.
- Inform those responsible for dealing with the customer complaint of the complaint.
- Actively listen to the customer by asking questions to clarify their concerns. When they have finished, paraphrase or summarise their main points to demonstrate that you listened and to check that you accurately understand their problem.

- Identify with how they are feeling, "If that happened to me I would be really annoyed. I'm sorry this has happened."
- Inform the customer of what you intend to do to resolve the problem.
- Provide some appropriate compensation to the customer for the inconvenience suffered.
- Direct the customer to someone who can solve their problem when you can't.
- Remember that customers pay your salary - avoid becoming angry or upset when customers make complaints. Think - "opportunity to turn a situation around", not, "complaint".

- Remember that the customer is frustrated at the product or the service or the organisation, not you personally, but at this moment you are the focus of their frustration.
- Provide privacy as many people find it embarrassing to complain.
- Identify what can be said to customers which will help them feel better.
- Practise responding to customer complaints during staff training sessions.
- Ask other staff what they think and do to handle customer complaints successfully - learn from each other.
- Follow through on customer complaints to check that the customer's problem has been resolved.

Moments of truth

Customers are probably getting a little weary of the constant barrage of advertising attempting to convince them that the customer is number one, that the customer's needs are paramount, that customer service reigns supreme over all other concerns.

Advertising doesn't convince a customer of the quality of the service he or she receives - experience does. Through the moments during which they actually experience your level of service - moments of truth - customers form their perceptions about the quality of customer service provided by your organisation.

Here are a number of points aimed at improving customer service that managers can discuss with their staff:

- Discuss the concept of 'moments of truth'.

- Ask staff to identify 'moments of truth' for their customers. For example :
  - waiting time in queues.
  - the response they receive from staff when they make an enquiry.
  - the response they receive from staff when they ask 'ignorant' questions.
  - the response they receive from staff when they ask for things beyond the normal.

    - the response they receive from staff when they make a complaint.

    - the visual impression your office or shop or place of business creates.

    - the response they receive from staff when they ask for information about the product or service.

    - how we recover when we have caused a problem.

    - how they are treated by staff.

    - how the product or service meets their expectation.

- Discuss the idea of 'recovery' versus 'blame'. This is how we respond when a problem occurs especially when we are at fault and even when we haven't been the cause. How do we go out of our way to recover the lost ground in the eyes of the customer? What do we do at this point which is exceptional even if it costs? Or do we go down the 'blame' path? For example. An important customer has requested some information about one of our products. The customer waits three days and for whatever reason, the information doesn't arrive. The customer (fortunately for us) rings to ask about the requested information. 'Blame' response, "We did post that to you three days ago. Gee, the postal service is slack. I'll post it again today." 'Recovery' response. "We did post that to you three days ago. Gee, I'm sorry, that's annoying. I'll get on to this right away and courier it to you within the next 30 minutes. I'll call you to check that you have it."

- Discuss the concept of 'creating advocates' out of our customers. If we meet our customer's expectations, we have a satisfied customer. If we exceed our customer's expectations, we have an advocate - somebody who will speak favourably about us to their family, friends and acquaintances.

- Ask what can we do which will exceed our customers' expectations? Make up a list of 10 key actions which will exceed customers' expectations. Get the team to agree that over the next two week period we will all focus on doing these actions. Meet again in two weeks time to discuss how each team member went. Ask each person (including yourself) to discuss verifiable examples of what they did and how the customers reacted. Continue this as a standard practice.

There's more than one way to skin a cat

> **"** Our problems are man made, therefore they can be solved by man. And man can be as big as he wants. No problem of human destiny is beyond human beings.
> **John F. Kennedy**
> *Address, The American University,*
> *Washington, D.C. June 10, 1963*
>
> Problems are only opportunities in work clothes.
> **Henry J. Kaiser (1862-1967)** **"**

The most common failing in decision making is to jump to the first obvious solution. To "do it now!" is a commendable philosophy, but only after the desired outcome is very clear. It should be added that perhaps the second most common failing is not to make a decision at all.

We make decisions to solve problems. Here is a step-by-step approach to solving problems and making decisions.

STEP ONE: Identify and define the problem
- Beware of snap judgements
- Don't mistake a symptom for the problem
- Sift back through the symptoms to find the cause
- Look for the root cause - ask "why, why, why?"
- Brainstorm ideas for identifying the problem

STEP TWO: Analyse the problem
- Obtain the facts of the problem (who, what, where, how, why, when)
- Seek opinions / attitudes and beware of assumptions and inferences
- Explore any constraints that may exist
- Check for underlying or hidden causes

STEP THREE: Define desired outcomes
- Be clear about what you want to see happen

STEP FOUR: Identify alternatives
- Generate a number of alternative solutions
- Be creative and innovative - think laterally, hypothetically, out of left field
- Keep an open mind - accept all options at this stage
- Don't overlook simple alternatives or the alternative of doing nothing
- Consider involving those who will implement the decision

STEP FIVE: Evaluate alternatives and decide
- Weigh up the pros and cons of each alternative discarding any which will not achieve the objective
- Consider the consequences of the decision you make on all stakeholders
- Consider factors such as feasibility, company policy, ethics, resource availability and cost, likely opposition, level of authority needed for implementation, who else will be affected, what could go wrong, what further problems could be created and staff acceptance

STEP SIX: Act on your decision
- Remember that change can be disturbing to staff and customers.
- Plan how your decision will be implemented (who, how, what, where and when)
- Communicate with all those affected by the decision in advance of the implementation stage - make sure you give reasons and answer any questions truthfully
- Work at getting active support and participation

STEP SEVEN: Follow up and evaluate the decision
- Don't let your ego make you blind to unsatisfactory results
- Correct errors and modify the decision if necessary
- Maintain contact with those involved to provide support and to follow through on suggestions, requests, etc.
- Ensure that the objective is achieved
- Note successful ideas to use again and errors to avoid

Delegation not abdication

Are you constantly running out of time - failing to meet your deadlines? Maybe you are ineffective at managing yourself or maybe you need to transfer more responsibility and authority to some of your staff.

Delegation does not mean dumping routine, boring and unpleasant tasks on staff. It is an action designed to give staff greater responsibility and to push authority and decision making down to lower levels in the organisation.

Beware - not all staff want more responsibility and authority. However, when handled properly, most people respond well to added responsibility. You need to assess the skill and will of your staff prior to delegating. Remember that ultimate accountability always rests with you.

The prerequisites for effective delegation are:
- A willingness to trust staff and to accept the risks involved.
- A willingness to relinquish some power and control.
- A degree of commitment, motivation and capability on the part of staff.
- A belief that part of a manager's job is to develop the competence and commitment of staff.

WHY DELEGATE?
Does the output (quality and quantity) of your staff lessen in your absence? Do your staff constantly refer problems to you? Do you have enough time to concentrate on your highest priorities? Are decisions made at the lowest level at which

they can effectively be made? Are you optimising the full potential of your staff? Do you spend too much time putting out fires, dealing with crises demanding your personal attention, and coping with the irritating details of day-to-day problems which keep you from working on the major issues?

When delegating follow these guidelines:
- Assess the skill and will level of the individual concerned before you decide to delegate.
- Explain why you have chosen this person for this task or project.
- Describe the task or project.
- Describe the required outcomes and the consequences on all stakeholders, not how to do the task.
- Clarify required quality and safety standards.
- Discuss why the task or project is important.
- Specify the person's level of authority.
- Discuss the nature of the support and resources you will provide.
- Discuss a time frame.
- Clarify how progress is to be monitored and the end result checked.
- Ask them to summarise the points of your discussion.
- Indicate trust by letting them get on with the job - without interference from you.

> I never had a boss that tried to sit on me, and I think that's essential. If you expect people to develop, you have to give them the responsibility, you have to tell them what their objectives are and you have to let them do it
> **David M Rodman**
> *Chairman U.S. Steel, Sky, June 1,1984.*

Fear and loathing in the workplace

One of the greatest obstacles to improving profitability and productivity in organisations is fear. Not the fear associated with physical threats, but a much more subtle and even deadlier fear that strangles creativity, creates distrust, blocks improvement, endangers lives, promotes stagnation, reduces quality and kills motivation. People are loathe to be open and honest about issues affecting productivity, quality and safety because they fear the consequences.

In fact, the effectiveness of some of the management strategies described in this book will be severely reduced if fear is a pervasive force in the organisation. Managers need to be aware of this powerful force which operates as an undercurrent beneath the surface of everyday organisational life. What are some of the things people are fearful of in the workplace?

Reprisals or repercussions

People fear that if they really do speak their mind when they are encouraged to do so by management they will suffer some negative consequence. Staff know that some bosses, despite what they say, really don't want to hear views which differ from their own. The negative consequences can take many forms from the obvious (being overlooked for promotion) to the subtle (missing out on rewarding jobs or development opportunities).

Nothing will change

"Why bother? Nothing will change." This is the catchcry of the disgruntled worker who has lost all faith in management's will and ability to change the things which, from the worker's perspective, are stupid, obsolete or unnecessary.

Damage to their reputation

In some organisations, staff know that one mistake is a lifetime sentence. It's safer and better to stay in the comfort zone. Don't make waves. Toe the management line. Tell the bosses what they want to hear.

Reactions from the boss

The manager invites feedback from team members about things for which the manager is accountable. The manager can't handle criticism and rationalises any feedback into nothingness or becomes vindictive. The relationship with the manager is damaged and work becomes an unpleasant experience. The team member is rejected by the manager. Or the manager reacts badly to bad news or to concerns about the viability of a project the manager is pushing. So staff learn to suppress bad news or perceived negativity and let the manager find out the hard way when it's too late to prevent a catastrophe.

Reactions from their workmates

Team members who make suggestions to improve things are often ostracised by their workmates. They are seen as 'sucking up' to management or of attempting to 'feather their own nest'. Peer group pressure is an extremely powerful force in the workplace. The team member is rejected by other team members.

Being ridiculed.

In the absence of a full understanding about the situation, a team member makes a valid (to them) suggestion which is treated with disdain by the manager or other team members. The team member is embarrassed or hurt and quickly learns to keep their thoughts on ways to make things better to themselves.

Is the glass half full or half empty?

As has been established many times in this book, people's perceptions dictate their behaviour and fear is one of the strongest forces within the organisation working against change or improvement or creativity or innovation. The process below can be used by a manager and the team to improve problem solving, make better decisions, implement required change or as an analytical tool.

To achieve these things, a manager needs to create an environment where people will willingly and honestly express their perceptions.

Groundrules
1. All views are acceptable.
2. All views are treated as important to the person expressing them.
3. All people are encouraged to express perceptions.
4. Contradictory opinions are encouraged.
5. Radical opinions are encouraged based on sound rationale.
6. Conservative opinions are encouraged based on sound rationale.
7. No ridicule of other people's perceptions.
8. No repercussions for expressing perceptions.
9. Facts are to be separated from assumptions and opinions.
10. People can comment on every or any question or statement.
11. Each of the four categories must be used.

The questions or statements are used in relation to the proposition under consideration, the planned change, or the decision to be made.

Perceived Negatives
- These are things it doesn't appear to take into account...
- This is why people won't like it...
- This is the message it conveys to our people...
- This is the message it conveys to our customers...
- This is why I am uncomfortable with it...
- This is why it may not work...
- These are the things working against it...
- My concerns about what we are doing are...
- The risks involved are...
- This is where we disagree...

- This is what I fear...
- This is what others fear...
- These are the obstacles...
- These are the constraints...
- This is my gut reaction to it...

Perceived Unknowns
- These are the assumptions we are making...
- What are the things we need to know more about?
- These are the unknowns...
- What are the 'what if...' scenarios.
- What is the likely impact on all stakeholders?
- What are the opportunities?
- How would we overcome identified obstacles or constraints?
- What is likely to change in the future which will affect this?
- What are the hidden or underlying issues which could block this?

Perceived Positives
- This is what I like about it...
- This is what our people would like about it...
- This is what our customers would like about it...
- These are the values it demonstrates...
- This is the message it conveys to people...
- This is what is innovative or creative about it...
- Here's what has worked well before about it...
- This is why it could work...
- These are the known facts...
- This is my gut reaction to it...
- These are the things we agree...
- These are the opportunities...

What Needs to Happen
- These are the conditions necessary to make it work...
- This is how it needs to be sold...
- This is what would have to happen for me to commit to it...
- This is what would have to happen for other people to commit to it...

Don't say "don't"

Feedback is about providing information to staff on their performance - about how they are going. When providing feedback, it is easy to fall into the trap of focusing only on the negative. To use the word "don't" has some interesting ramifications.

Firstly, it produces a degree of resentment from the person to whom the feedback is being directed. Secondly, it focuses only on what the person shouldn't do and consequently does not provide any specific instruction or information about what they should do. Next time somebody says "don't" to you, take time out to think of how you respond, how you feel, what you think and whether you know what corrective action to take.

Here are some things you can say which will help you provide constructive feedback in a way that is quite acceptable to the recipient. Don't forget, feed them with positives every time. (Did I say 'don't'?) There are five points to consider.

- **What they should do more of**
  "This is great work I'd like to see you do more of this."
  "Well done, I would like to see you do it this way every time you do this job."
  "If it could be done to this standard every time it would be great. I would be really happy seeing you do more of this."

- **What they should continue doing**
  "Keep this up. This is exactly how we want it done."
  "I am really pleased. Keep doing it this way because it makes the work easier for all of us."
  "Do exactly what you are doing now. This is really getting the results we want. Great work."

- **What they should start doing**
  "Good work. Now you have got this far I would like you to start doing.............."
  "What you have done so far is very good. The next step to do is............. which

is what I would like you to do the next time we are working on this project."

"Let's start doing this now, seeing that you have really got a good understanding of the first part."

FEEDBACK.

- **What they should do less of**

"What you have done so far in this area is what I want. When you are doing this bit try to do less of this and it will help reduce problems later on."

"We've got this bit right. Next time try doing a little less of that and you will find it a great help."

"To make life easier for you and to get the job done more quickly do less of this bit."

- **What they should stop doing**

"If you stop doing this it will speed up the process considerably."

"Did you know if you do this and stop doing that it makes a big difference to the accuracy?"

"Good work in this section here. Next time try to resist the temptation of doing this and the whole thing will be perfect."

Good grief!

All organisations have situations which result in dissatisfaction for one or other parties. Where a problem remains unresolved and one party feels aggrieved, it is important that management handles the grievance in a fair and objective manner.

One would hope that applying the 'grievance policy' is a rarity because the working relationship is often permanently damaged when a grievance gets to this stage. The manager must be seen to be fair and unbiased for they too can be dragged into the mire of the conflict.

Consider these tips to help resolve genuine grievances in the workplace.

- Establish an organisation grievance procedure (if one does not exist) and inform all staff members of its existence and the requirement to use this process should a grievance arise.
- Form a grievance committee comprising management, workers and union representatives.
- Familiarise yourself with the organisation's official grievance procedures.
- Follow the established grievance procedure when a grievance arises.
- Consider the industrial implications before the process begins.
- Set up a mutually acceptable time for the grieving parties to meet.
- Identify which people will be required to provide information to the grievance committee.

- Ensure all stakeholders have an opportunity to state their case.
- Document the reported grievance and the actions taken to date.
- Gain agreement about what the grievance is.
- Gain a commitment from all parties to reach a resolution.
- Gather all the relevant information by asking questions and listening to the answers. Ask who, what, when, where, how and why.
- Sort fact from assumptions and seek verifiable evidence of information provided.
- Seek the opinions of other relevant staff before making a decision.
- Ask, "What needs to happen to resolve this issue fairly?"
- Brainstorm alternative solutions with the parties in conflict.
- Make a decision based on fairness and fact and not assumption.
- Discuss the impact the grievance is having on the rest of the organisation.
- Discuss the impact the decisions may have on the organisation before announcing them.
- Negotiate a mutually acceptable solution.
- Make the necessary decisions to address the grievance, i.e. don't delay in making a decision.
- Make provision in the budget to address substantiated grievances if necessary.
- Respect the confidentiality and rights of all parties involved.
- Consider the impact inaction may have on the rest of the staff.
- Seek advice from colleagues who may be more experienced in grievance handling and resolution processes.

First impressions stick

Sweating palms, sweaty under arms, rapid pulse, butterflies in the stomach, nervous laughter.... all symptoms of the first day at work. Can you remember your first day at work? Can you remember your first day in your current job? What were you thinking? How did you feel? How long did it take you to find out vital information about the organisation and what your job entailed?

Why do we induct new staff? Some of the key benefits in inducting new staff properly are greater productivity earlier, enhanced workplace satisfaction and it enables them to fit into the team more quickly and easily.

Someone needs to assume responsibility for the induction of new staff into the organisation. Usually this rests with the line manager.

The new staff member will be far happier if the person carrying out the induction follows these tips.

- Prepare an induction plan.
- Introduce the new staff member to other staff with whom they will be working near or with.
- Prime other staff to be welcoming and enthusiastic.

- Introduce them to all management with whom they will come into contact.
- Provide a list of names and locations of colleagues to help the new person remember who's who.
- Welcome the new staff member publicly.
- Arrange for a guided tour of the organisation.
- Explain the basic, vital ways things are done at your organisation, e.g. messages, leave, security, stationery, parking, safety requirements, emergency evacuation procedures, etc.
- Provide a 'buddy' for the new staff member. Someone who is competent and has a positive attitude.
- Demonstrate how to use organisation equipment, e.g. phone, photocopier, fax, binding machine, email, etc.
- Show them where all equipment is kept.
- Ensure that their work station is clean, tidy and prepared.
- Clarify your expectations of them for the first month.
- Discuss what support you will provide in this first month.
- Provide a key to their work area.
- Discuss organisational strategic priorities.
- Explain our key products and services.
- Explain how our organisation is structured.
- Discuss issues unique to the organisation environment and customers.
- Provide them with important contact numbers - yours, security.
- Provide them with a schedule of organisation 'events' which occur on a regular basis.
- Provide time for the inductee to absorb the information they have been given.
- Set aside time for the staff member to ask questions after they've been at the organisation for two weeks.
- Inform them of the normal communication procedures.

A good start

Use this checklist to help with staff induction.

Induction Checklist

PERSON RESPONSIBLE FOR INDUCTION:		
EMPLOYEE NAME:	**JOB TITLE:**	**START DATE:**
INDUCTION NEEDED		**COMPLETED/COMMENTS**
1. Introduction to organisation - general background information about the company.		
2. Policy on: • smoking • parking • what to do if you are late or ill • signing on / signing off - time sheets		
3. Details of: • award / workplace agreements • job description • contract of employment • payment method and procedures • superannuation (occupational) / sick leave entitlements • hours of work / possible or likely overtime • break times - lunch, morning and afternoon tea		
4. Tour of premises including location of: • lunchroom / canteen / eating area • toilets / bathroom • other recreational facilities • warehouse • service area • office and administration areas • production		

INDUCTION NEEDED	COMPLETED/COMMENTS
5. Introduction to relevant managers / staff / co-workers. • Description of other related operations / names of staff with whom they may come into contact.	
6. Sources of advice and assistance in the company.	
7. Health and safety requirements. • location of first aid kit • location emergency exits / evacuation routes • introduction to the safety officer/warden • location of fire extinguishers • emergency numbers and call signals	
8. Quality assurance. • summary of quality assurance • description of all procedures relating to them and relevant work instructions	
9. Details about and issuing of: • IT equipment • safety equipment, e.g. hard hat, glasses, ear muffs • tools likely to be used • other equipment - e.g. phone, fax, photocopier • supplies including stationery, ordering process	
10. On-the-job training required (List below)	

'Us' versus 'them'

> One man may hit the mark, another blunder;
> but heed not these distinctions. Only from the alliance of the one,
> working with and through the other, are great things born.
> **Saint-Exupery**
> *The Wisdom of the Sands (1948), tr, Stuart Gilbert*
>
> Clapping with the right hand only will not produce a noise.
> **Malay Proverb**

Within how many organisations does their exist an 'us' versus 'them' mentality? Observation suggests it exists to varying degrees in almost all organisations. The reasons may stem from many factors - historical conflict, differing education levels, lack of understanding of roles, duties, functions and work practices, an inability to see the value to the organisation of the other area, differing pay structures and so on. The reasons may well be based on jealousy and the perceptions of "I am working harder than them", "Our section is of more value to the organisation than theirs", "They are getting more than me."

Lack of co-operation between areas and the negativity which results feed off each other. One way to break it down is to acknowledge the worth of all areas and consciously look for the value the people in each area add to the whole organisation. Consider how effective the organisation would be if one or other area didn't exist. How would it affect your job and the jobs of your staff? Developing and maintaining harmony requires a high degree of consultation before improvements in co-operation between areas can be made.

A great deal of energy can be wasted in the 'obstructive' mode in organisations.

INTERDEPARTMENTAL CO-OPERATION

Channelling this energy into a positive force can ensure that the organisation becomes a more productive and far happier place in which to work.

- Identify areas in the organisation which rely on your area to function at its optimum level and vice versa.
- Assess the effectiveness of the working relationship between the separate areas through conducting staff surveys and observation.
- Identify specific situations which require better co-operation and then discuss the importance of and need to improve interdepartmental co-operation where it is identified as a problem.
- Discuss the causes of poor co-operation between departments.
- Ask other managers how you can assist their department to function more effectively.
- Ask your staff what assistance they require from other departments to help them to function effectively.
- Inform other areas of your needs and requirements to enable your area to function properly.
- Inform staff of the co-operation requirements of other areas.
- Discuss what changes are required in the way we operate to improve interdepartmental co-operation.
- Identify and discuss how we can implement ways to improve co-operation.
- Explain to other department managers what you will be doing to improve interdepartmental co-operation.
- Acknowledge the actions of other departments which have responded to your requests for co-operation.
- Implement new ways of doing things to improve interdepartmental co-operation.
- Provide staff with feedback from other departments in relation to any changes they have made.
- Reward and provide recognition to individual staff who make efforts to improve interdepartmental co-operation.
- Discuss with senior management the actions you require from them to help you improve co-operation between departments.

What you put out you get back

Work is more pleasant and productive if a manager builds and maintains good relationships with staff. Easier said than done. Let's face it, there are some people who you will inherently dislike. Putting aside your prejudices is not easy and once a relationship is damaged it takes a lot of understanding, enlightenment and will to repair.

There will always be a few hardheads who may be too damaged by past experiences to see that their behaviour is actually counter-productive and that by winning they are really losing. However, most people respond reasonably when they perceive that you are treating them reasonably. Sometimes you have to look for the butterfly not the grub.

FIVE WAYS TO BETTER RELATIONSHIPS

1. Work on your self concept
- Remind yourself that you are an important human being. Accentuate the positive aspects about yourself. Allow yourself to be imperfect and make errors and fail occasionally - everybody you know does, why not you too? Remember we learn more from our 'failures' than from our successes. You can't always be right all of the time.

2. Listen with three ears
- Have a purpose for listening.
- Look at the person.
- Suspend judgement initially.
- Ignore distractions. If distracted - apologise, explain that you got distracted and ask them to say it again.
- Wait before responding.
- Paraphrase to the speaker's satisfaction.
- Be on the lookout for the important themes of what the speaker says.
- See the world from their position.
- Reflect on the content of what you hear and search for meaning.
- Be ready to respond.

3. Be clear and precise in your expression

- Remind yourself that the other person is not a mind reader.
- Don't leave people guessing about what you mean.

4. Cope with angry feelings

- Be aware of your feelings - don't deny or suppress them.
- Observe the strength of the feeling and its source.
- Overcome the urge to say things which are fuelled by anger. Wait until you have a calmer and clearer perspective. Most things said in anger are regretted later.
- Accept responsibility for what you do.
- Talk about how you feel. Make no accusations.
- See the connection between your thinking and your feelings.

5. Be ready for self disclosure

- Talk fully and truthfully about yourself. Treat with respect what other people tell you about themselves.

Walk the talk

Some more ideas on improving interpersonal relationships.

BUILD TRUST

- Be predictable and reliable.
- Communicate clearly. Avoid saying you will do things you don't intend to do. Be clear about whether you are making a commitment or just talking about possibilities.
- Take your promises seriously. Write them down and act on them. Review them regularly.

HELP OTHERS TO BE MORE RELIABLE

- Don't overload trust Take action which reduces risk, e.g. avoid leaving money lying around.
- Trust others when they deserve it. Don't let your aversion to risk or perfectionism or need for control stop you from delegating.
- Be specific in praise and criticism. Give feedback which is fair, accurate and about specific behaviour. Use verifiable examples.

TREAT PROBLEMS AS OPPORTUNITIES, NOT CRIMES

- Use each incident of apparent unreliability as an opportunity to reduce the likelihood of it happening again.

MIND YOUR MANNERS

- Don't talk about colleagues behind their back. If you do, what do you think the person you are telling is learning about you?
- Treat all your staff fairly. Don't delegate the good jobs only to your favourites.
- Praise in public and criticise in private.
- Remember common courtesies like please and thank you.
- If you discover that you are wrong, adjust your mistake and apologise.
- Give credit when its due to the source. Don't put forward other people's work or ideas as your own.
- Treat all people regardless of status with respect.

> If (a man) is brusque in his manner,
> others will not co-operate. If he is agitated in his words,
> they will awaken no echo in others. If he asks for something without
> having first established a (proper) relationship,
> it will not be given to him.
> **I Ching**
> *Book of Changes, China, c. 600 B.C.*
>
> Civility is not a sign of weakness,
> and sincerity is always subject to proof.
> **John F. Kennedy, 1917-1963**
> *Thirty-fifth President of the United States,*
> *Inaugural address, 1961*

Resume the position

An essential manage-ment tool is a job or position description. It needs to be up-to-date, accurate and informative. Here is a guide for preparing a position description.

Position Summary
- Why does the position exist? Why is the position needed? What is the major outcome of the job, i.e. what is the main thing the job is meant to achieve?

OR

- What are the major task areas or what are the major results the position should produce?
- Title of immediate supervisor?
- Number of people reporting to this position?

Position Duties and Responsibilities
- What are the main tasks or activities which must be carried out in doing this job? How do you go about doing these things?
- Write statements incorporating what is done and how it is done. Write the statements in order of priority. Which is the most important task? Which is the next most important task? etc.

Position Requirements
- Knowledge - What things must be known to enable a person to do this job?
- Skills - What skills (actions) must a person be able to perform to do the job?
- Abilities - What physical or mental activities must the person be capable of to do the job?

Minimum Qualifications
- What are the minimum education or trade requirements?
- What are the minimum experience requirements?
- What are the minimum training requirements?

Limits of Authority
- For what activities necessary to do this job are you required to gain the approval of your immediate manager, e.g. expenditure above a certain amount, dismissal of staff, hiring of staff, use of equipment, etc?

Client and Supplier Relationships - Internal and External
- With which other key people do you have regular interaction in your work? What is the purpose of these interactions? To do what? To obtain what?
- What information, materials and services does this position provide and to whom?
- What information, materials and services does the position receive and from whom?

Key Performance Indicators
- For each major task or activity ask - if a person was performing this task successfully, what concrete things would you see happening? How would you know? What evidence would there be?

Some managers think that job descriptions are a waste of time. If that is you, here is simple alternative. On one or two pages, state clearly the following using two columns.
1. Outcomes I expect you to deliver.
2. My expectations about how you will deliver each outcome.

Any questions?

When you are interviewing a candidate for a job, are they likely to tell you anything which will show them in a poor light? Unlikely. Will they try and tell you what they think you want to hear so that you will select them for the job? Of course.

One of the factors which determines the success of a recruitment interview is the ability of the manager to ask probing questions. Questions which make the applicant demonstrate that they are the best person for the job.

Good interviewers constantly probe an applicant's answers for facts, verifiable examples or precise meaning. Remember that the candidate will attempt to put a good spin on everything.

Unless you are checking on details in their resume, avoid asking questions that can be answered by yes or no. Here are a range of questions you might ask in a recruitment interview.

- What assets do you bring to the job? What are your best qualities? What qualities do others see in you?
- What are your shortcomings? What areas do you need to develop or improve? What qualities do you wish to develop further?
- What constructive criticism have you received?
- How might you be a risk for an employer?
- What things have you done best? Done less well? What things have you liked best? Liked less well?
- What are your major accomplishments? How did you achieve them? Describe your most difficult problems and how you handled them?
- In what ways are you most effective with people? In what ways are you least effective with people?
- What have you learned about yourself from your work experience?
- What is the key to managing people? Or fitting in with people?
- How would your present boss describe your assets and liabilities? How would your friends describe your assets and liabilities?

- What will be your main challenges in this job? How would you spend your first week or two in this job?
- What verifiable examples can you give to back up your claims?
- How do you like to spend your spare time? What social activities do you take part in? To what extent are you involved in the community?
- How would you describe your home life? How do you feel about your current financial status? What are your goals in life?
- How would you compare your attitude to work with that of the average person in this country? What factors mainly influence your motivation at work?
- How would you describe the best boss you've ever had?
- How would you describe the worst boss you've ever had?
- Why would you be able to perform successfully in this job?
- What skills or knowledge have you gained which will be required in this job?

Round peg. Square hole.

> Here lies a man who knew how to enlist into
> his service people better than himself.
> **Andrew Carnegie**
> *American industrialist and philanthropist, Epitaph.*
>
> Obviously the interviewer learns little or nothing when he is talking.
> **John D. Drake**
> *President, Behavioural Sciences Technology,*
> *Interviewing for Managers (AMACOM,1972)*
>
> A man is not always what he appears to be,
> but what he appears to be is always a significant part of what he is.
> **William Gaylin**
> *Psychiatrist, Columbia University, The New York Times, Oct 7, 1977*
>
> The World's great men have not commonly been great scholars,
> nor its great scholars great men.
> **Oliver Wendell Holmes 1809-1894**
> *American physician and popular writer,*
> *The Autocrat of the Breakfast Table.*

Probably the most critical interview that a manager conducts is the selection interview. Choosing the wrong person for the job can have disastrous consequences in terms of cost, loss of customers, productivity, your own reputation and the effect on other staff.

Some things to consider in conducting selection interviews :
- Unless the situation requires a pressure interview, create a relaxed, supportive atmosphere. Reduce the initial anxiety of the applicant by engaging in some small talk regarding a hobby or some aspect of their work experience

mentioned in their resume.

- Allow that nervousness at an interview does not necessarily mean that the person would not be able to perform well in the job. Some of the most competent and capable people on the job actually show up poorly at interviews.
- State the purpose of the interview - for the candidate to demonstrate that you should select them for the job - the format it will take and the role of others if it is a panel interview.
- Prepare and use a candidate assessment form which lists essential and desirable criteria, weightings, ratings and score. Complete your assessment and make your notes immediately following each interview. Make a note of their dress or a physical feature to remind you later of who was who.
- Plan the interview in advance and maintain flow and direction during the interview. Prepare statements and questions in advance and ask them clearly.
- Remember to maintain an appropriate ratio of talking to listening - about 30:70 in their favour.
- Listen to what the person is saying, how they are saying it, how well they listen to your questions by their response, and for feelings behind what they are saying. Paraphrase, summarise and reflect their answers when you want more information.
- Listen for generalisations and probe them for specific details.
- Keep asking them to verify any claims they make.
- Sort through irrelevant answers by asking the applicant to explain how it relates to this job.
- Ask open-ended questions which make the applicant think and continually probe for specific examples or justification.
- Remind the applicant that the onus is on them to demonstrate that they are the best person for the job.
- Be aware when your own biases are affecting your judgement. A person you dislike for a variety of reasons may be a top performer in the job. Idiosyncrasies which annoy you might have no effect on others.
- Ensure that you have asked all the questions from your list and that the applicant has no further questions.
- Indicate clearly the next course of action to be taken.

Sell yourself or else

If there is ever one time in your life when it does not pay to be humble, it is when you are being interviewed for a promotion or a job. This is the time to promote yourself and sell your features, advantages and benefits. Don't rely on the interviewer to ask you the right questions to bring out your strong points. There are good interviewers and bad interviewers.

Don't get the wrong idea. Bragging is to be avoided. Just demonstrate with verifiable examples how and why you meet or exceed the selection criteria for the job. You don't know the selection criteria for the job? If you can't find out beforehand by asking the person conducting the interviews, then analyse the job advertisement and list the criteria you would have to demonstrate to win that job.

Don't like selling yourself? Tough. Because if you don't who will? It is not the interviewer's role to convince herself that you are the best person for this job. That's your role. And don't rely on your resume. That really only gets you to the interview. Everybody can look good on paper. And while I'm at it, don't rely on your referees. It's good to be able to nominate referees as opposed to not being able to nominate a referee - but that's about all they're good for.

No one ever nominates a referee who won't speak highly of them. Your best referees are your previous bosses and long standing customers. Don't nominate your long term 'drinking buddy'.

Now if you're half way normal, you'll be nervous before and possibly during the interview so if you prepare thoroughly you will feel less nervous and increase your chances of winning that job. One way to prepare is to consider what the interviewer is looking for during an interview.

The interviewer will be most impressed by the candidate who can:
- provide verifiable evidence that they are the best person for the job.
- demonstrate (as far as possible) during the interview that they can meet the selection criteria.
- get on with people and fit into the organisation and work group.
- demonstrate honesty.
- demonstrate reliability.
- demonstrate their experience in resolving likely problems associated with the job.
- analyse a question before answering.
- demonstrate good listening ability by responding to the question asked.
- express their opinion clearly.
- provide evidence of achievements in previous jobs relevant to the criteria.
- back up any claim they make.
- ask intelligent questions about the job and the organisation.
- demonstrate a stable job background or can explain why they may have had many jobs.
- readily provide answers to questions to show they are prepared.
- answer hypothetical questions.
- display knowledge of the organisation.
- show a genuine interest in the job.
- show potential to advance to a higher position (possibly).

Can you judge a book by its cover?

It is said that interviewers make up their minds about a candidate for a job within the first 4 minutes of a job interview. They then spend the rest of the interview looking for evidence to reinforce their impression.

This can make it tough for the candidate who might not impress at first sight, but would be quite capable of doing the job well.

Most professional recruiters are aware of this 'first impressions' tendency and are able to resist the impulse to make an early decision. They stay objective and continue to look for verifiable evidence of the candidate's suitability for the duration of the interview.

Here are some things to say and do to help create and confirm a positive impression:

- Arrive 5-10 minutes early.
- Sell your features, advantages and benefits - don't rely on your achievements to speak for themselves or the fact that it is all in your resume. Be aware that the interviewer may not have absorbed all the information contained in your resume.
- Give a brief summary of the reasons why you can excel in this job, even if not asked.
- Demonstrate with examples your personal attributes, e.g. honesty, reliability, trustworthyness, hard-working, etc.
- After answering a question, ask "Have I satisfied your question?"
- If you don't understand a question, state your interpretation of the question and ask if that is what they mean.
- If you don't know how to answer a question, say "I don't know from experience, but my opinion is...." Don't try to bluff your way through an answer.
- Wear neutral clothing.
- Don't rely on the interviewer to ask the appropriate questions.
- If you are nervous (everybody is) don't calm your nerves with alcohol.
- Maintain normal, direct eye contact without glaring or staring.

- Tell the interviewer the true reason behind your separation from an employer.
- Be yourself because that's all you can be.
- Refrain from swearing, complaining about your current or last job.
- Check that - your nails are clean, your breath is fresh, your teeth are clean (no food stuck between them) your hair is neat (no dandruff), your deodorant is working.
- Articulate clearly by focussing on how you are saying word beginnings and endings - avoid slang like 'gunna' (going to) or 'dunno' (don't know).
- Thank the interviewer for their time and the opportunity to meet with them.
- Check that a follow up response to the interview has been discussed.
- Demonstrate your knowledge of the organisation and your enthusiasm to work there.

Captain, my captain

There are some managers who are better leaders than others. What do they do that sets them apart from the pack? Is it a natural set of qualities they possess or can we learn to be better team leaders?

All good captains possess an understanding of the technical issues and demonstrate an ability in this area. They also have an innate ability to be able to rise to the occasion in times of adversity. More importantly, however, they understand and manage the human and conceptual issues which influence their team mates.

Here are some very specific things you can do which will help you be a better team leader:

- Ask staff to identify ways to improve team work.
- Implement new, better and different ways to improve team work.
- Allow all team members to contribute to decisions.
- Identify team members strengths and utilise these to the benefit of the whole team.
- Seek regular feedback from team members about your actions and how effective they feel you are in managing the team.
- Clarify the role and authority of each member of the team making sure each person knows exactly what they have to do.
- Convey unpopular decisions to the team by providing the rationale for the thinking behind the decision and the benefits to the team
- Involve team members in establishing team goals.
- Discuss the benefits of staff working together as a team.
- Provide clear direction to the team by holding regular team meetings, discussing the objectives and purpose of the team's work.
- Identify the nature of the support, team members require from you, and provide it.
- Ensure that communication within the team is accurate, timely and relevant.
- Act to resolve any conflict within the team.

- Provide feedback on team results.
- Speak positively about the team by pointing out things they have done well.
- Avoid asking team members to do things you wouldn't do yourself.
- Demonstrate the types of behaviours you wish team members to adopt.
- Demonstrate consistency when handling team issues by displaying the same response to the same situation but at the same time being aware of individual differences.
- Discuss team successes and the contributions of team members.
- Recognise and reward outstanding teamwork.

IVAN THE TERRIBLE   ALEXANDER THE GREAT   RON THE MEDIOCRE AND HAPPY JUST TO FOLLOW ALONG

Nothing stays up without support

OFFER SUPPORT...

One of the key functions of managers is to make work life easier for their staff. You don't agree? We're not talking about doing their work for them, but creating an environment which will be supportive of what they are trying to achieve. Think through some of the benefits to you? Less interruptions, people knowing what to do, increased job satisfaction, higher productivity, more profit and so on ....

The demands of work are changing all the time and there are requirements of staff that they too make changes to the way they do things. If there is an expectation by management for change to take place then a 'structure' that will support these changes must be provided.

You as the manager need to be looking for new, different and better ways of doing things to facilitate this change.

Give some thought to these:
• For each new change, list the support requirements staff are likely to need. Consider things like training, time to implement the change, resources required, communication requirements.

- Ask staff what support they believe they need and identify the priority of these.
- Identify the types of support you believe staff may need during the planning stage of any new project and ask staff to write down the support they think they will need.
- Conduct a training needs analysis and then develop and document a training plan that will address the requirements of staff.
- Provide emotional support when a need exists particularly where staff appear to be stressed or suffering from problems at home. Do this by giving them the opportunity to talk to you about their problems. Just talking is sometimes all they need.
- Budget for the things that have been identified as important.
- Offer support in areas you believe staff may need assistance. They may not want it but the offer is still made.
- Seek assistance from external sources when appropriate and prepare submissions to apply for this support.
- Make yourself available to support staff and colleagues. Consider this to be part of your role as manager and not something extra which is taking you away from your 'real' work.
- Seek professional development for yourself to enable you to provide the support to staff that they may require.
- Take into consideration that each individual has different needs for support. Evaluate their individual abilities - their strengths and weaknesses - and then plan accordingly.
- Meet to discuss staff support requirements whenever there is change or you identify a problem.
- Consider the confidentiality and sensitive nature of some support requirements staff may have. Sometimes there are issues which others need not know about or may be embarrassing to the staff member concerned.
- Ask other managers about situations where support might be needed.
- Ask staff to describe what they would like you to do more of or less of to support them.

The lights are on but nobody's home

> "To be able to really listen, one should abandon
> or put aside all prejudices...When you are in a receptive state of mind,
> things can be easily understood...But, unfortunately, most of us listen
> through a screen of resistance. We are screened with prejudices,
> whether religious or spiritual, psychological or scientific; or, with daily
> worries, desires, and fears. And with these fears for a screen,
> we listen. Therefore we listen really to our own noise,
> our own sound, not to what is being said.
> **Jiddu Krishnamurti**
> *Indian philosopher and writer*
> *The First and Last Freedom (Harper, 1954)*

One of the simplest and most sincere compliments you can pay somebody is to show that you are listening to them - hearing the message they intended.

Most of us would describe ourselves as good listeners. But are we? Unless we have a hearing impairment we can listen and hear noise. Yet what we actually hear is more to do with our mind than our ears.

One sure way to kill commitment and motivation is to show your staff that you don't really listen to them. Not by what you say, but what you do. If you want your people to listen to you, show that you listen to them.

There is nothing magical about being a good listener. Good listeners are better at concentrating - staying focussed on the message of the speaker. They have the ability to overcome internal (mental) and external distractions. People with over inflated egos make poor listeners. Nothing the speaker is saying could be more important than what they are thinking.

These are some of the things which distract our minds when listening :

- Preconceived ideas about the topic - established mindsets.
- Thinking about an unrelated thought triggered by the speaker.
- Selective hearing - only hearing what reinforces your point of view.
- Thinking about something said that you didn't understand
- Dislike of the topic or the speaker.
- Tuning out because you don't value the opinion of the speaker.
- Assuming you know what the speaker is going to say.
- Wanting to jump in and respond immediately.
- Taking offence at something that was said.
- Thinking about what you will say when the speaker stops speaking.
- Fabricating a story in your mind to massage your ego. (Concocting lies)
- Reacting to a mannerism or something about the person's dress.

A manager can employ some simple techniques to develop active listening skills:

• **Paraphrasing:** Repeating back to the speaker the essential meaning of what has been said. For example, "What I hear you saying is..." "Do you mean that...?" "So in other words are you saying...?"

• **Reflecting feelings:** Describing or acknowledging how the speaker might be feeling. "I'd feel frustrated too if I was in your position."

• **Summarising:** Briefly summarising the key points the speaker has been making. "So in summary, are you saying that...?" "Well, your main concerns seem to be..."

To actually use these simple techniques forces you to actively listen. By doing so you will develop greater understanding of other people's thoughts and feelings and demonstrate that you are really listening and hearing.

It takes guts, but ask them

I've never yet met a manager who believes that they do a lousy job as a manager. I've met hundreds of staff who believe that their manager is incompetent as a manager. (And yes the converse applies as well). How does a manager know how well she is managing her people? One way to find out is to ask the people who are being

managed. Simple, but scary. Probably not a good idea for the egomaniacs (they would dismiss any negative feedback anyway) or those managers with low self-esteem.

On the other hand, it is not an easy process for staff either. Should I be honest? How will he take it? Can she handle it? Will he hold it against me? Will I suffer in some way?

Some managers believe (incorrectly) that to ask staff for this sort of feedback about their own performance destroys their credibility. Every manager can benefit from holding a 'Management Review Meeting' every six months with their staff.

Here is a process which can make this easier for both the manager and your staff. Explain that you would like constructive feedback about your performance as a manager. Ask your staff to complete the following five statements.

To enable me to achieve my objectives and to perform my job more effectively, I would like you (the manager) to :

1. CONTINUE DOING these things.... (here they describe things you do which help them to do their job and which they would like to see continued).

2. DO MORE of these things....(Here they list things you do occasionally, but which they would like to see you do more often).

3. START DOING these things....(Here they list those things which would help them do their job more effectively, but which you aren't currently doing).

4. DO LESS of these things.... (Here they list those things which you do which impede their ability to perform their job effectively, but which you do for other reasons).

5. STOP DOING these things.... (Here they describe those things which cause them to be ineffective or to lose motivation and for which they believe that there is no valid reason)

To make this process one of equal participation, the manager can complete the same statements in relation to staff. During the meeting, the manager and staff make note of the actions described during this exchange, discuss reasons for current actions and make commitments for change.

Fact or fiction?

> **"** Knowledge is of two kinds; we know a subject ourselves,
> or we know where we can find information upon it.
> **Samuel Johnson**
> *Quoted in Boswell's Life of Samuel Johnson, April 18, 1775.*
>
> Every step by which men add to their knowledge and skills is a step
> also by which they can control other men.
> **Max Lerner**
> *'Manipulating Life', in the New York Post, Jan. 24, 1968.* **"**

Management information systems are the 'steering wheels',
'rudders', 'handle bars', 'compasses' of organisations. Without
them we could head in any direction and not really know why
we went there or how we got there.

Identifying a problem that needs addressing is usually left to a 'gut feeling' or
'professional judgement'. However to effectively resolve the problem, we need
verifiable evidence about the nature of the problem and the need to do something
about it. Never ignore your intuition.

Management information systems are a means by which we gather data and
collect information which in turn enables us, through analysis, to determine the
status of the area under review. Once we have done this we can then turn our
attention to 'fixing' the problem. It is no longer just based on the 'gut feel', but
hard evidence as well.

- Identify the specific areas for which information will be required.
- Identify the specific needs for information of both the organisation and
  the work teams within the organisation.

MANAGEMENT INFORMATION SYSTEMS

- Discuss with staff what management information systems are and the benefits to the organisation of using them.
- Define and discuss the key performance indicators for your area.
- Discuss and agree with staff the best means of gathering information.
- Discuss alternative means of gathering information.
- Train staff in how to gather the information.
- Identify the people for whom information will be required.
- Identify the areas from which information will be gathered.
- Analyse the results to determine common trends.
- Prepare reports which provide evidence of results and summaries of the statistical data collected.
- Express data in a graphical format.
- Seek staff opinions on information gathered.
- Display information and data for staff to consult and discuss.
- Discuss the findings with staff.
- Prepare a plan to address these needs.
- Resource the plan according to need and current organisation priorities.
- Keep records of all data collected and decisions made.
- Compare the information collected against your performance indicators.

A necessary evil?

A common complaint from managers and staff is the number of meetings they have to attend which consume valuable time. Meetings are necessary, but they don't have to be perceived as a waste of time. No one will complain if a manager sets out to reduce the quantity and improve the quality of meetings.

A good place to start is to compare the meetings you conduct against this list of reasons why meetings attract such bad press. This analysis of your own meetings will highlight ways that you can improve the quality of your meetings.

WHY MEETINGS FAIL

Here are some of the more common reasons why meetings are too often seen to be ineffective:
- Decisions made at the meeting are not followed through to implementation.
- Poor or no preparation by the meeting leader and the participants.
- 'Hidden agendas' - people have other issues usually related to self-interest which are not related to the purpose of the meeting.
- Non-attendance of key people so that decisions have to be put on hold.
- Lack of control by the leader so that the conversation wanders into areas that do not add value to the purpose of the meeting.
- One person dominating discussion and decisions so other people present don't bother contributing their ideas.
- The meeting leader has a pre-determined outcome - no consensus.
- No one has the authority to make the decision.
- The reason for the meeting was not strongly established in the first place.
- The outcome or the decision is not really agreed - people go along with the decision, but with no real conviction.
- The reason for the meeting or the purpose of the meeting is not established or is unclear.
- People are not committed to the reason for the meeting.
- There is a lack of emphasis on fact - more focus on opinion, assumption and inference.

- People don't feel safe to say what they really think and feel.
- People of lower rank feel intimidated by those of higher rank.
- Contributions are not sought and obtained from all participants.
- Lack of stability of the meeting participants, i.e. key people being replaced while on leave or other business by people who have no background knowledge of a particular agenda item.

- The counter-productive or negative attitudes of some participants are not confronted or brought out into the open.
- Insufficient notice about the meeting.
- No action plan with a monitoring process agreed in relation to decisions made.
- No check of the level of commitment of participants to a decision.
- No clear agenda established with priorities and time allocations for each agenda item.
- No circulation of an agenda with clear identification of how participants will be expected to contribute to the purpose of the meeting.
- Meeting starts late and finishes late.
- Too many items/activities planned for the time available.
- Illegible or poor quality visual aids.
- No evaluation of how effectively we conduct our meetings.

Meetings, meetings, meetings...
and more bloody meetings

Many meetings are a waste of time! I'm sure we don't need to remind you of that. If the best decisions are not made in a time frame which is reasonable it is due to one of these things:

- **poor meeting structure**
- **poor leadership or**
- **poor participation**

As the chairperson or participant we have responsibilities before, during and after the meeting.

Meetings represent the best available communication and consultative process for maximising effectiveness and improving organisation productivity.

BEFORE THE MEETING

- Inform participants in written form, of meeting details, such as time, venue and agenda.
- Provide opportunities for all staff to contribute to the agenda.
- Select a time of the day to hold the meeting that allows participants to give their undivided attention.
- Circulate the objectives of the meeting and the input required from participants.
- Limit the number of objectives to those that can be achieved within the time available.
- Ensure you are prepared in the areas for which you are responsible by thinking through the issues likely to be raised and plan your contribution.
- Appoint someone to record the key points and decisions reached during the meeting.
- Rotate the leadership role so that other people develop the confidence and competence to conduct effective meetings.
- Estimate the amount of time needed to discuss each objective.
- Prepare an 'action plan' sheet for each person's use.
- Set a time limit on the meetings duration.
- Plan ways of making the meeting interesting by using aids, charts, transparencies, activities, etc.

- Check aids such as overhead projectors are working.
- Prepare a summary of what actions or tasks were completed, as was agreed at the previous meeting.

DURING THE MEETING
- Start the meeting on time, even if some people aren't present.
- Control the discussion by nominating who is to talk, and when.
- Open the meeting by clarifying objectives, format and expectations.
- Encourage participation by ensuring that every person's contribution is heard.
- Ask questions of non-contributors.
- Make 'hidden agendas' the subject of a separate meeting.
- Ensure that all discussion is relevant to the stated objectives.
- Ask talkative members to clarify how their comments relate to the objectives.
- Record on the action plans who does what, how and by when, etc.
- Separate facts from opinions and assumptions.
- Encourage consensus when making decisions.
- Summarise the key points of a discussion to ensure clarity of issue and decision.
- Check the level of commitment to the decision.
- End the meeting on time, regardless of whether objectives are achieved.

AFTER THE MEETING
- Spend time discussing ways to make meetings more productive.
- Counsel disruptive participants pointing out the consequences of their actions on the meeting.
- Distribute a record of the minutes of the meeting.
- Follow up on agreed actions with staff responsible for completing those actions.
- Agree with staff the amount of time needed to conduct future meetings.
- Prepare a summary of what was agreed to at the meeting.

You can make a difference

It is not just the meeting leader who can make or break the success of a meeting. Sure, the leader has prime responsibility, but the participants have a key role to play in making meetings effective.

It is a good idea for a manager to establish some ground rules to govern the way all participants conduct themselves at meetings. In fact, if you want to improve the quality of your meetings, call a meeting to review the effectiveness of your meetings. The establishment of agreed ground rules during this meeting will be one step toward successful meetings.

Here are some ground rules for participation to get the ball rolling. It is important that you establish your own with your team and that everyone is committed to follow them.

GROUND RULES FOR PARTICIPATING IN MEETINGS
- Pay attention and respond to others people's ideas and feelings.
- Allow others to finish what they are saying - don't interrupt.
- Make open ended enquiries - ask who, what, why, how, where and when.
- Accept other points of view as legitimate for them - don't judge people.
- Use active listening techniques such as paraphrasing or summarising to reflect back others ideas and feelings.
- Allow free expression - no manipulating or controlling of other people's ideas and feelings.
- Speak in friendly terms - avoid sarcasm and put downs.
- Evaluate the ideas not the person.
- Create opportunities for other thoughts and feelings to be expressed.
- Accept that everybody has perceptions which might not be grounded on fact but are nonetheless important to them.
- Separate fact from opinion, assumption and inference.
- Build on the ideas of others - extend them further.
- Encourage and allow different points of view.
- One person speaks at a time.
- Focus all conversation on the problem-solving process.

- Question own and other peoples' assumptions in a non-threatening way.
- Declare all assumptions about an issue.
- Ask people to give verifiable and specific examples of generalisations.
- Ask people to openly state their level of commitment to a decision or a particular course of action.
- Review every meeting for success and effectiveness.

Silence is compliance

I cannot devine how it happens that the man
who knows the least is the most argumentative.
Giovanni del Cassa, 1503-1556.
Papal Secretary of State, Galateo.

Because the executives don't say what they really mean
or test the assumptions they really hold, their skills inhibit a resolution
of the important intellectual issues.... Thus the meeting ends with only
lists and no decisions.... People's tendency to avoid conflict,
to duck tough issues, becomes institutionalised and leads
to a culture that can't tolerate straight talk.
Chris Argyris
Harvard Graduate School of Education.
Harvard Business Review, September/October 1986.

At times during meetings the participants are reluctant to talk. This may be due to a host of reasons; lack of knowledge of the topic, being intimidated by the situation, fear of being seen as stupid, unwillingness to express an opposing point of view for fear of causing conflict..... Whatever the reason the chairperson, you, will need to generate discussion. Here are some things you can say to do this.

- **Ask questions that help to draw people out and express their ideas.**
"What is your reaction to ....?"
"What are some other ways to .....?"
"What do you think would happen if.......?"
- **Paraphrase.**
"So what you're saying is........."
"Before we go on, do you mean that........?"
"Let me see if I've got it right. You mean......."
- **Involve quiet people.**

"Mary, what do you think about this?"

"Can you tell the group what you were saying about this to me last week Hon?"

"I'd like to hear what Bill has to say about this."

• **Ask for examples.**

"Will you give me some examples of the type of thing you mean please Erica?"

"Tell me what things happened in your area Jose."

• **Conduct a quick survey.**

"Can I see a show of hands on this?"

"What is the general feeling about this issue?"

"Let's hear what the group have to say."

• **Ensure clarity.**

"You look puzzled Ted. Would somebody like to explain how this will work in Ted's section?"

"Could somebody explain to May Lee just how this will affect what she is doing in her department."

• **Confront differences.**

"You look as if you don't agree Sue. Speak now or for ever hold your peace."

• **Question assumptions.**

"Your idea assumes that staff won't be happy with what management have suggested. Is that right?"

"What you are saying will happen may not actually affect the others as much as you think."

• **Be supportive.**

"Let's give Gustav a chance to explain what he means."

"It's great that you have made a suggestion about how we should tackle this problem Kia. We need to explore this line of thinking further."

• **Make procedural suggestions.**

"What we will do is deal with this issue first and then handle that point next."

"We need to clear up this point before going on because the decision is going to affect all sections."

• **Seek solutions.**

"How should we proceed from here then?"

"What do you think is the best way to handle this one given all the facts before us?"

• Check for consensus.

"Before we go on does every body agree that ...."

"Am I right in thinking we all support this way of doing it? If you have reservations I welcome them. Let's hear of any concerns. "

"How many of you are fully committed to this?"

A voyage of self discovery

> People learn from their failures.
> Seldom do they learn from their success.
> **Harold Green**
> *Chief Executive Officer, IT&T Managing (Doubleday 1984)*

The concept of mentoring is one which is becoming a more accepted form of personal and professional development in the workplace. The purpose of mentoring is to assist the learner to learn and develop through insight, awareness and discoveries prompted by the discussion between the mentor and the learner.

Being a mentor is not the same as being a role model. A manager can be a role model without being a mentor. And vice versa.

Mentoring is characterised by the use of 'understanding' seeking questions which allow the learner (and the mentor) to arrive at their own understandings. It is a two-way process which provides learnings for both the mentor and the learner.

The mentor acts as a facilitator and a catalyst for learning rather than as a 'teacher'. The learner is responsible for her own learning. The mentor is responsible for supporting, facilitating and learning with the learner. Interestingly, the mentor does not need to be a technical expert in the job function of the learner.

Key points about mentoring:
- The mentoring process can be applied in various contexts - a workplace assignment as part of a training program; a special project or major task which has been delegated to the learner; a skill deficiency which has been identified; or when the learner has made a major mistake.

- Focus on the learner's understanding more than just doing a task.
- Seek to understand the causes of any problems before moving to resolution.
- Use paraphrasing as part of active listening.
- Avoid the "you should do" statements.
- Focus on getting the learner talking as opposed to you talking.
- Ask questions which show the learner that you are curious about the answer or solution.
- Focus on achieving understanding - not teaching.
- Focus on using 'understanding seeking' questions (see 'Let the Penny Drop')
- Show empathy by describing how you felt in a similar situation.
- Encourage them to describe the situation from the perspective of others.
- Adopt a neutral point of view.
- Re-direct a question if you get no response to the original question.
- Avoid accepting generalisations as answers to questions - ask for their specific experience and how that has formed their view.
- Tolerate mistakes - use them as opportunities to learn.
- Seek common ground and/or use common interests to develop the relationship.
- Allow time for the learner to develop - move at their pace.
- Assess what the learner knows - don't assume they know.
- Conduct mentoring on their territory or in a neutral place.
- Avoid discounting their ideas - use them to springboard into other ways of thinking.
- Use hypothetical questions - "If.... what would you do?"
- Recognise the different realities of the learner - their perception may differ from yours.
- Discuss the roles and responsibilities of the mentor and the learner.
- Allow the learner to arrive at solutions and decisions.
- Focus on improvement - what would the learner do new, different or better next time.
- Both mentor and learner should evaluate the effectiveness of the mentoring process continuously. Use these questions of each other:
  - What am I doing which you find unhelpful?
  - What am I doing which you find helpful?

Lead from behind

Socrates, the Greek philosopher who died in 339 BC, was declared to be the wisest man of his time in the world. He is described as philosophically representing, at the highest, values of questioning and discussion without bigotry or preformed conclusions, thus exposing feeble arguments and prejudices. (Guthrie, W.K.C. (1971). Socrates. Cambridge.)

The Socratic method of teaching and learning is employed in the mentoring process. Here are some more things to consider for a manager acting as a mentor.

- Establish ground rules regarding when to let the learner 'fail' and when the mentor will intervene and rescue the learner from some undesired consequence.
- Discuss what gains are expected by both parties.
- Record key issues and points for future reference after each meeting.
- Allocate effective preparation time for mentoring sessions.
- Demonstrate your commitment to the mentoring process by ensuring regular mentoring sessions - schedule meeting dates and times.
- When beginning a mentoring process, reach agreement on how the mentoring

process works - agree the conditions that make mentoring effective.

- Acknowledge any shortfalls you may have in knowledge and experience of the mentoring process.
- Hold a 'kick off' meeting to establish and agree the purpose, the outcomes, the process, the conditions, your role and their role.
- Conduct the mentoring sessions on their territory or on neutral territory.
- Explain that you are a partner in the learning process and that you expect both of you will obtain new insights and knowledge.
- Discuss how the learner will cope with any changes to their workload associated with the mentoring process.
- Allow the learner to learn by experiencing the consequences of their own actions.
- Use positive reinforcement - acknowledge right efforts as much as right results.
- Identify opportunities for both parties to learn - share your learnings with the learner, but don't let this take up too much air time.
- Create a climate where the learner can experiment and discover without fear.
- Use role playing as a tool for learning.
- Employ plenty of silent moments to allow the learner time to think and arrive at their own conclusions.
- Allow and encourage the learner to become more skilled than you.
- Check for understanding of communication given and received.
- Recognise and work on correcting inappropriate behaviour and help them see better ways of thinking and doing.
- Take time out to review the effectiveness of the mentoring process from both points of view.
- Review agreed actions within agreed timeframes.
- Be prepared for spontaneous opportunities for mentoring - a continuous process.
- Determine whether any extra training may be required.
- Let the learner decide and act on their decisions.
- Continue to display leadership by making decisions when required - do not abdicate decision making responsibility when needed.

Let the penny drop

Mentoring is a subtle skill which allows the learner to create their own 'aha's'. The manager's main tactic as a mentor is to ask a range of questions to let the learner arrive at their own realisations or learnings. These questions require the learner to express the level of understanding they have in relation to the situation. Or the level of awareness, or insight or learning they have currently attained.

These questions allow the learner to process their experience of the situation - to evaluate the experience, to use deeper thinking or higher level thinking. This in turn leads to new ways of thinking and doing and the development of new competencies.

Here are a sample of the types of questions a manager might ask of the learner when acting as the learner's mentor.
- What things happened during this project/task which you didn't expect?
- What was different about this project/task from other projects/tasks?
- What were your reasons for making that decision?
- What insights did you gain from this experience which you would use in a similar situation?
- What would happen if you were to do it that way?
- How else could you look at this situation?
- How would people react to you if you were to do that?
- What worked for you this time that didn't work for you before? How would you explain that?
- What things did you learn which you didn't expect to learn?
- How would you compare the difficulties in this project with the difficulties in the XYZ project?
- How did other people react differently to you? How would you explain that?
- What would you change about what you did if you had to do it again?
- How will other people react to what you propose? What would be their reasons for reacting that way?
- What are the implications of this experience on future situations?
- What do you think my reasons would be for suggesting an alternative

to your proposal?

- Where are the opportunities for new ways of doing things in this project?
- What are the underlying forces that are driving this situation?
- What conditions have changed over this period of time?
- What things are not what they appear to be? How are they impacting on this problem or situation?
- How would the situation change if you were to remove this factor....?
- Who else might be stakeholders beyond the ones you have identified?
- What other consequences might be considered beyond the ones you have identified?
- What other factors might be causing this situation beyond the ones you have identified?
- How would you have to change to be more effective next time?
- What would your proposal convey about you, to other people?
- How would you have to think differently to deal with this problem differently?
- How might your current ways of thinking about this be limiting your actions?

WHAT WOULD YOU THINK ABOUT HAVING PORK FOR DINNER TONIGHT?

HOW ELSE COULD YOU LOOK AT A SITUATION?

The big picture

Chief executives and senior management are expected to understand the 'big picture'. It won't hurt if all employees have a better understanding of the big picture. At the very least, they will better understand the rationale behind some of the decisions made by senior management which they have to put into action in the workplace.

Managers interested in informing their staff about the big picture can discuss the answers to some or all of these questions with staff :

• What is our core business?

• Who are our major customers or users? What are our main markets, outlets or distribution channels?

- What are our main products or services?

- How has our business changed from what it was five or ten years ago? How has the environment in which we operate changed or how is it likely to change in the near future? What should be different about our business five to ten years into the future?

- What are our main economic concerns?

- Where does our main income and capital come from?

- What things are important to our organisation in relation to our image, leadership in industry, the community, the environment, marketing, equal opportunity, innovation, risk-taking, quality, management style, culture, etc.

- What special considerations do we have in relation to owners or shareholders, parent organisation, employees, customers, suppliers, the general public, unions, legislation, government?

The ideal way to communicate this information is to hold short briefing sessions with small groups of staff. The answers to these questions should be confined to no more than two to three pages and distributed to staff at the session.

The main purpose of the briefing session is to allow discussion of this information. People should be encouraged to ask questions.

Most people respond positively when they see that the organisation makes serious and effective efforts to keep them informed.

Skill is nil without will

> It is not the martinets that make an army work;
> it's the morale that the leaders put into the men that
> makes an army work.
> **Harry S. Truman 1884-1972**
> *Thirty-third President of the United States.*
>
> Sadness diminishes or hinders a man's power of action.
> **Benedict Spinoza, 1632-1677**
> *Dutch philosopher and oculist, Ethics.*
>
> Productivity is closely tied to morale, and morale is a reflection
> of how people see themselves. If you can improve your employees'
> perceptions of themselves, you can improve their morale -
> and thereby boost productivity.
> **Howard Hurst**
> *President, Memphis Personnel Association,*
> *Personnel Journal, March 1986.*

Morale is about self confidence, pride, self image, passion for the cause, determination to succeed, motivation, support, zeal, willingness, contentment, recognition of achievement, celebration of success, etc.

A manager can do these things to improve staff morale :

- Identify the causes of low morale - ask staff.
- Allow team members to express their feelings about things upsetting them.
- Ask staff to suggest things we can do to improve morale.
- Discuss with senior management the causes of low morale.
- Seek input from all team members on decisions which affect their work.

134

- Take action with people in the team who are not carrying their load.
- Identify opportunities for team members to learn new skills from other team members.
- Distribute boring, routine work evenly throughout the team - share the load.
- Rotate jobs among team members.
- Discuss ways to make the work more creative, challenging and fun.
- Look for opportunities to provide recognition and feedback.
- Acknowledge 'right efforts' as much as 'right results'.
- Identify the expectations and perceptions of team members concerning the degree of recognition and feedback that they receive.
- Discuss ways to provide recognition and feedback.
- Involve team members in goal setting, planning and decision making.
- Ask for people's opinions on things - people like to feel valued.
- Show team members that their opinion is valued by acting on their ideas and suggestions and giving them the credit.
- Involve team members in the 'big picture' and show how their work contributes to the welfare of themselves and their work mates.
- Delegate jobs to team members which give them new challenges and opportunities to develop.
- Allow team members who are doing boring, routine work opportunities to let off steam or express their boredom. Be more flexible in allowing opportunities to socialise.
- Hold regular meetings to discuss problems, needs and concerns of the team
- Allow a degree of flexibility and choice about how team members achieve their work objectives.
- Set targets and create competitions for team members related to work output.
- Celebrate successes and important events.
- Look for opportunities to provide support to team members who need it and then provide it.
- Encourage open communication by treating all perceptions as important.
- Recruit staff who have a positive attitude and are enthusiastic about their work.

What cheeses me off

> Everyone has noted the astonishing sources of energy
> that seem available to those who enjoy what they are doing and find
> meaning in what they are doing.
> **Charles Garfield**
> *President, Performance Sciences Corp. Peak Performers (Avon, 1986).*

> Whoever would change men must change the conditions of their lives.
> **Theodore Herzi, 1860-1904.**
> *Austrian journalist and Zionist leader, Diaries.*

> Where there is no hope there can be no endeavour.
> **Samuel Johnson, 1709-1784.**
> *English lexicographer and critic, The Rambler.*

> Constant labour of one uniform kind destroys the intensity
> and flow of a man's animal spirits, which find recreation and delight in
> mere change of activity.
> **Karl Marx, 1818-1883.**
> *German political philosopher. Capital.*

People's perceptions of the environment in which they work have a huge impact on their level of motivation. A manager can discuss this checklist with his or her work group to identify possible actions to improve motivation of a work group.

Blockages to motivation:
- The physical arrangements at work are unsatisfactory.
- People believe the wages or salaries are unfair.
- I do not feel secure about my job.
- The organisation has not helped my personal development.
- Higher management is not concerned with my views.

- There is little real interest in my job.
- My job is meaningless.
- The work environment is depressing.
- Annual leave arrangements are unsatisfactory.
- I fear for my long term job security.
- People fear repercussions if they are open and honest.
- Most people here have little opportunity to gain new experience.
- I would like to be consulted more when decisions are made which affect how I do my job.
- My job has no clear targets.
- The colour schemes, lighting and general decor are bad.
- I would like more feedback about my performance.
- Employees know too little about organisation aims and plans.
- I would benefit from being extended more in my job.
- The organisation does not try to develop jobs to fit individual needs.
- There is little effort made to provide social facilities.
- Organisation decisions don't take in the needs of employees too.
- My training has rarely been well planned.
- There is no systematic effort to identify and incorporate employees' views.
- I am not given new responsibilities even though I could handle them.
- The workplace is poorly cleaned and maintained.
- Product competitiveness is poor, affecting the company's long term prospects.
- I should like to have a clearer personal development plan.
- Most people feel uninvolved in decision making.
- Food service arrangements and facilities are below standard.
- Our remuneration compares unfavourably with other organisations in our industry sector.
- If I were to leave, I feel that the company would not miss my contribution.
- I don't feel that my contribution is acknowledged.
- Insufficient effort is put into developing people's skills.
- There is a strong 'us and them' attitude among managers and staff.
- I am often bored at work.

If you show me yours, I'll show you mine

Successful negotiators believe that everything is negotiable. Is it? There are situations where this may not be so, but it is a useful attitude to adopt. Obviously, the manager who believes everything is negotiable is less likely to give up in the face of strong opposition than the manager who does not hold this belief.

Here are some tactics for conducting successful negotiations. The range of choices open to both parties and the type of consequences you are prepared to accept will determine which tactics you choose. Be careful - what you put out you'll get back eventually.

- Be direct. Know what it is that you want and ask for it.
- Allow plenty of time to conduct negotiations. Don't put pressure on yourself which may cause you to seek less than you need. Rushed decisions are usually poor decisions.
- Promote trust by demonstrating your willingness to co-operate especially early in the proceedings. Look for other options. Attempt to make all parties feel that they can win something. Declare a desire to seek win/win outcomes.
- Ask the other party to state their opening offer first.
- Make your first requests high, but within the limits of the other party's ability to meet your requests. State your major requests at the beginning and use the minor issues as options for later trade-offs. Introduce unimportant issues as important ones and concede them later to give the other party a sense of gain.
- Ask the other party to join with you in resolving the issue. Ask how you can assist them to meet their needs. Ask them how can they assist you to meet your needs.
- Ask them to explain the rationale behind unreasonable requests.
- Ask them how their requests are fair to all parties and/or all stakeholders affected by the possible outcomes.
- Show how your requests are fair to all parties and/or all stakeholders affected by the possible outcomes.
- Test the climate by asking hypothetical questions. What if....? Suppose that I were to....? Say if you were to....? What would happen if we were both to ....?

If I was prepared to do.... would you be prepared to do....?

- Propose suggestions which advance the negotiation.
- Respond to their proposals with counter proposals.
- Re-present your same proposal but in a different form - one which incorporates the expressed interests, requests and limitations of the other person.
- Clarify time limits, financial limits, limits of authority and any other limits early in the negotiation process. Set conditions before making offers.
- Trade requests - exchange things you need for things they need.
- State the benefits for them if they accept your proposal.
- Combine an unacceptable request with a request that they are likely to concede. Make one conditional upon the other.
- If close to achieving your objectives, but in a deadlock situation, suggest that you split the difference.
- Overwhelm the other party with lots of information so as to end their argument before they begin.
- Identify the objections the other party holds and explore with them the reality of these things happening.
- Say, "If you do this ....then we have a deal".
- Agree what you have agreed - summarise it and write it down.
- Agree on an action plan.

Give away the wool, not the sheep

> The old idea of a good bargain was a transaction
> in which one man got the better of another. The new idea of a good
> contract is a transaction which is good for both parties to it.
> **Louis Dembitz Brandeis, 1856-1941**
> *U.S. Supreme Court Justice, Business - A Profession*
>
> Never get angry. Never make a threat. Reason with people.
> **Don Corleone**
> *The Godfather*
>
> He who will not reason, is a bigot; he who cannot is a fool;
> and he who dares not is a slave.
> **William Drummond, 1553 -1610**
> *Scottish Poet, Academical Questions*

Negotiation is a vital management skill in today's industrial and commercial environment. Managers need to be able to negotiate with their employers, their employees, union representatives, buyers, suppliers, customers, government officials and the general public.

Every day in a manager's life, something will require negotiation. It is a constant part of successful management and is a characteristic of enlightened cultures.

Negotiation usually involves looking for compromise - finding solutions which reasonably meet the needs of both parties. In fact, when one party is not prepared to work for compromise, negotiation usually breaks down.

Never lose sight of the big picture. Today's concession might be tomorrow's gain. Are you winning the battle but losing the war?

As with most things in life, preparation is the key to success. Here are a number of things to do before you begin to negotiate:

- Clarify the matters to be negotiated. What is, and what is not, up for negotiation?
- Define your objectives - from those you would like to get through to those you must get.
- Establish the desirable outcomes for both parties. List the maximum objectives - what would be the ideal result for both parties? List the minimum objectives - the point at which neither party will accept anything less.
- Put a priority on your objectives. Anticipate the priority the other party will put on their objectives.
- Consider what concessions you might make and what you require in return.
- List the facts you know about the situation. Separate facts from assumptions. Check the validity of your assumptions. What assumptions might the other party make?
- Decide what information you require and what information you are going to disclose.
- Research in detail all your facts. Sort out inferences and opinions. Make sure the information you present is irrefutable. Identify those facts which will help your case and weaken the case of the other party.
- Decide how the other party will use the facts about the situation and prepare points to counter them.
- List the issues for you and the other party. What are the common issues, hidden issues, and non-issues?
- Divide issues into major and minor, difficult to settle and easy to settle, monetary and non-monetary, long term and short term.
- On each issue decide your position and that of the other party.
- List their perceptions about the situation and the basis for these perceptions.
- Determine what you would need to say or show to change their perceptions to ones more favourable to your objectives.
- Define personal needs and wants and organisational needs and wants for both parties.

Beauty is in the eye of the beholder

What did you see when you first read the sentence in the triangle?
Paris in the spring? Well, if that's what you saw then maybe you
better do what you've been threatening to do for years and get
those peepers checked. Wait a minute. If you saw 'Paris in the spring',
don't panic. It's got nothing to do with your eyesight. It is to do with what
is referred to as 'selective perception'. By now you will have realised that
the sentence above reads 'Paris in the the spring'. One 'the' too many.

If you ask people when seeing this for the first time to write what they see, most
people will write 'Paris in the spring'. They leave out the second 'the'. Selective
perception - your mind perceives only that which makes sense to your mind. Your
mind is trained to recognise a complete sentence. Simply put, the second 'the'
does not make 'sense' to your mind, so your mind ignores it.

Relating this to people, you see in people what it is that you want to see in people which supports your image of them. If you dislike a person, you will tend to
see their behaviour in a certain light - unfavourably. If you like that person, you
will tend to see their behaviour in a different light - favourably.

Perceptions play a powerful part in the behaviour of people at work. A person's
perceptions dictate their behaviour - what they will and will not do. The root cause
of most problems in the workplace is frequently the different perceptions of the
people concerned.

People hold perceptions about themselves, about their manager, about their team members, about their role, about their priorities, about how well they do their job (everybody believes of themselves that they do a 'good' job), about what is right and what is wrong, about what makes sense to them and what doesn't, about their rights, about your treatment of them, etc.

People's perceptions are formed from their life experiences, their conditioning, their value system, etc. and their knowledge or awareness of the issue at stake. We can change people's perceptions by broadening their awareness - giving them new ways of thinking about things - if they have the will to change.

To identify and broaden people's perceptions about an important issue, try the following :

- Explain that it is important that we express and clarify the different perceptions that we all might hold about the issue.
- Explain that we need to suspend judgements about what is right and wrong and that everyone's perception is a reality for them.
- Say that the purpose of the exercise is to make a list of all the possible perceptions that people may hold about the issue.
- Encourage people to be honest and say that no one will suffer as a result of expressing perceptions that conflict with your own.
- Ask all team members to make a list of the perceptions that people may hold about the issue.
- Make a list of the combined perceptions of all team members.
- Go through the list one by one and agree which are based on fact and which are based on assumption or inference.
- Ask people to explain the rationale for or against the perception by providing verifiable examples on which they have formed their perception.
- Check that everyone's opinion is listened to and the distinction between fact and assumption is made.
- Ask how people feel about the issue now that the facts are known.

Why don't they do what they're supposed to do?

> People's minds are changed through observation
> and not through argument.
> **Will Rogers, 1879-1935.**
> *American actor and humorist. Will Rogers (Hallmark, 1969)*
>
> All things are ready, if our minds be so.
> **William Shakespeare, 1564-1616.**
> *English dramatist and poet. Henry the Fifth.*
>
> It is extremely important that I know the other person is extremely
> receptive to what I'm saying. If he is not, then I will become a cause of
> the error if something goes wrong. I'm as much to blame as him.
> **Raymond Miyashiro**
> *CEO, Trans Hawaiian. Nation's Business, March 1988.*
>
> Behaviour is determined by its consequences.
> **B.F. Skinner**
> *Harvard University. Beyond Freedom and Dignity. (Knopf, 1971)*

Managing people becomes very frustrating when they won't do what they're supposed to do. People behave the way they do for a variety of reasons, some of which appear irrational and illogical. But to the person, their behaviour probably makes perfect sense.

Ultimately, people act according to how they perceive things not how you perceive things. Why don't employees do what they are supposed to do?

- They don't know why they should do it.
- They don't accept your reason for doing it.

- They don't place any value on the action.
- They don't perceive it to be important.
- They believe that doing it will make no difference.
- They don't know how to do it.
- They are angry about something and want to sabotage your efforts.
- They are under pressure from their workmates not to do it.
- They believe they will save time by not doing it.
- They believe that they will save effort by not doing it.
- They believe that they will avoid discomfort by not doing it.
- They don't know what to do.
- They think your way will not work.
- They think their way is better.
- They think something else is more important.
- They have nothing to gain by doing it.
- They think that they **are** doing it.
- They are rewarded for not doing it.
- They perceive that they are punished for doing what they are supposed to do.
- They anticipate a negative consequence for doing it.
- Nothing happens if they don't do it.
- Others don't do it.
- You don't do it.
- There are obstacles beyond their control.
- They don't have the confidence or competence to do it.
- They fear embarrassment or loss of face if they do it.
- They fear other people's reactions if they do it.

As good as it gets

The greatest of faults, I should say,
is to be conscious of none.
Thomas Carlyle
On Heroes, Hero - Worship and the Heroic in History (1841), 2.

The faultfinder will find faults even in paradise.
Thoreau
'Conclusion,' Walden (1854)

How will your staff know how they are going if you don't tell them? If you're going to tell them then how will you do it and what will you tell them? Are they going to believe you? Will it make any difference anyway?

There are two things we need to consider when appraising staff performance:

1. Positive feedback - which is given:
   a) when an employee is putting in a consistently good performance
   b) whenever an employee puts in an exceptionally good performance
   c) when an employee's performance improves after constructive criticism

2. Constructive criticism - which is given:
   a) when an employee's performance is less than standard performance.

The aspects of performance that need to be assessed are:
   • punctuality and attendance
   • safe work behaviour
   • care of tools, equipment
   • quality / accuracy of work

- quantity of output
- job knowledge
- dependability
- correct work procedures
- cooperation with employees / supervisor / manager

In addition to the ongoing feedback that managers give on an 'as needs' basis, formal performance appraisals are made every six to twelve months during a performance appraisal interview.

There should be no 'surprises' in the feedback given during the performance appraisal interview. It is an opportunity to review the previous six to twelve months on the job and plan for improvement in the future.

The Performance Appraisal Record
This is a written document which the manager completes before the staff appraisal interview. The staff member to be appraised also receives a copy of the document and is encouraged to complete it prior to the performance appraisal interview.

The Performance Appraisal Interview
This is a 'formal' interview in the sense that it is important, scheduled and has a definite purpose and structure. Managers use a Performance Appraisal check list (see 'Was it good for you too?') to guide the interview and plan improvement strategies.

The Follow-up Interview
Where necessary a follow-up interview is held after four weeks. This is done to review the progress of improvement strategies agreed to at the Performance Appraisal Interview.

Performance Appraisal documentation is filed and may be used when counselling, salaries, promotions, bonuses, or retrenchments are being considered.

Was it good for you too?

Before the interview:

- Complete the Performance Appraisal documentation before the employee's performance appraisal interview. This is done by the person who will conduct the interview. Normally, this will be the staff member's manager - you.

- Be fair to the person being appraised. Give yourself plenty of time to do this properly. A rushed preparation by you will indicate the degree of importance you attach to the process.

- Check that you understand the duties and requirements of their position before completing the form (see opposite page for a basic appraisal form).

- Refer to their job description if necessary.

- Assess each category separately. Unless you are careful, the 'halo' effect may influence your thinking. An employee who is excellent in one or more areas isn't necessarily excellent in all areas. Also, an employee who is below standard in one or two areas isn't necessarily poor in all areas. Your appraisals will be better if you are objective and analytical in the way you assess performance for each category. To be objective requires you to look only at the facts and then form your opinion from there.

- Separate quality and quantity. It is important that you don't allow a high rating for 'quantity of work' to influence your rating for 'quality of work'.

- Review each category independently.

- Avoid focusing only on recent behaviour or on single incidents. The review is for a chosen period and is an overall assessment of the staff member's work behaviour. Unless you are aware of the possibility, it is easy to let a recent poor or excellent performance influence your view of the total review period.

- Write in one or more examples of behaviour for each rating which is typical of the staff member's performance. Specific examples have more meaning to them than broad generalisations and they will help you to conduct better performance appraisal interviews.

PERFORMANCE APPRAISAL

EMPLOYEE:		JOB TITLE:				
MANAGER:		APPRAISAL DATE:				
Areas of Performance	OUTSTANDING PERFORMANCE	ABOVE AVERAGE PERFORMANCE	STANDARD PERFORMANCE	BELOW AVERAGE PERFORMANCE	UNSATISFACTORY PERFORMANCE	N/A
Punctuality and Attendance Comment:						
Safe Work Behaviour Comment:						
Care of Equipment Comment:						
Quantity/ Accuracy of Work Comment:						
Quantity of Output Comment:						
Job Knowledge Comment:						
Dependability (follows through on job) Comment:						
Correct Work Procedures Followed Comment:						
Cooperation (with employees / manager) Comment:						

Tell it as it really is

CHOOSE AN APPROPRIATE PLACE TO
CONDUCT THE INTERVIEW....

- Choose an appropriate time and place to conduct the interview. Performance appraisal interviews are important and should be conducted at a time and in a place which will do most to foster a worthwhile exchange of information.

- Avoid interruptions. The appraisal interview should be completed in one sitting. Take whatever steps are necessary to ensure that you and the employee will have at least 45 - 60 minutes of uninterrupted time.

- Put the employee at ease. Taking a minute or so to do this will help you to establish the right atmosphere for a worthwhile performance appraisal interview.

- Review each item on the appraisal document. While your aim is to discuss each item on the appraisal form, it is better if you avoid reading from it. Your aim is to create an atmosphere which is as friendly and natural as possible.

- Encourage discussion. As you review each of your main points, encourage the employee to give you his / her point of view. Ask them to provide reasons for their actions or examples of what they have done well. Ask them to suggest ways they could do their job better and what needs to be done by management to enable this to happen.

- Check to see if you will change any comments you made. If you decide to, do so there and then.

- Summarise the main points of the interview. After all the points have been discussed as fully as possible, summarise the employee's strengths and areas which need improvement. There should be agreement on what you write.

- Complete the appraisal documentation. This is an official document and needs to be signed and dated. It is also important that the employee feels free to write their comments in addition to any which you make.

- Explain the follow-up procedures. The employee needs to know that you will follow up on and record the progress of any improvement plans made during this interview.

- Close the interview. After covering all the items on the appraisal document, including a plan for improvement (if necessary) it is appropriate to ask if the employee has anything else they would like to talk about. It is also appropriate to:

  a) Reassure the employee of your interest in their progress, and

  b) Indicate your willingness to discuss problems or concerns at
     any future time.

When you have reached a natural stopping point close the interview on a positive note.

One bad apple...

> Friendly counsel cuts off many foes.
> **William Shakespeare, 1564-1616.**
> *English dramatist and poet, King Henry IV*
>
> Reason and emotion are each the other's counsellor
> and complement....Whoever takes counsel of one of them only,
> and neglects the other, is thoughtlessly forfeiting a part of the aid
> that has been granted for our guidance.
> **Marquis de Vauvenargues.**
> *French soldier and moralist, Reflections and Maxims.*

Counselling a staff member whose job performance is unacceptable is an uncomfortable process for both the manager and the person. Which is probably the main reason many managers avoid doing it. Here is a process to follow which will make it easier on both of you.

SETTING UP A MEETING
- Approach the person in private or out of earshot of others.
- Explain that you would like to meet with them to discuss their job performance.
- Explain that you will be doing this with other team members as well.
- Explain how you will prepare for this meeting and how you would like them to prepare for the meeting.
- Agree a specific time, date and place to meet in private.

PREPARATION (By the manager)
- List some areas of performance in which you would like the person to improve.
- List specific things that you would like this person to do new, different and better in each area.
- List the areas in which the person is performing effectively.
- List specific examples of things that they have done effectively.

PREPARATION (By the team member)

- List the aspects of their job which they think they do well. Cite a couple of examples in each aspect which demonstrates how effective they are.
- Identify aspects of their job which they think they could improve.
- Identify the specific things that they could do new, different or better in each aspect.
- Identify what other things would need to happen to enable them to make those improvements.
- Identify what training or coaching they require to make the improvements.
- Identify what they would like the manager to do more of or less of to help them make the improvements.

THE COUNSELLING SESSION

- Explain that this is an opportunity to improve the quality of work life for both of us.
- Say that all of us have different perceptions about various things that happen in the workplace and this is an opportunity for a frank and honest exchange of our perceptions.
- Explain how you will conduct this meeting - the format and your expectations.
- Discuss the areas of their job that they do effectively and the examples of specific things in each area.
- Ask them to discuss their view of the things that they do effectively.
- Reach agreement on the things that they do effectively.
- Discuss the areas in which you think they could improve and specify the things which you would like them to do new, different and better.
- Ask them for their view of what they could improve and the specific things they could do new, different and better.
- Agree a list of things for them to work on to show improvement.
- Discuss their view of the support they believe they need to make these improvements.
- Agree things which you (the manager) will do new, different and better to support their efforts.
- Agree what actions you will take to support them in the achievement of these improvements.
- Discuss your and their feelings about this session.
- Schedule a specific time, date and place to review how both of you have implemented your agreements.
- Thank them for their time and contribution.

Lead and lag?

As a manager, you will need to be able to measure the performance of your team in terms of quantity and quality of output. What are you going to measure?

The things you measure are called, 'performance indicators' - things which will indicate the performance of your team or work group. The main indicators of performance are called, 'key performance indicators' (KPIs). There are two types of performance indicators you can use - 'lead' and 'lag'. Lag performance indicators relate to outputs or results. Lead performance indicators relate to activities which, if they happen, will lead to the desired output or end result - lead up activities.

Most organisations are good at identifying and measuring lag indicators, but not so good at identifying and measuring lead indicators. A lag indicator will tell you whether or not you achieved the end result or output after the event. A lead indicator will tell you if you are likely to achieve the end result before it happens. This enables a manager to take corrective action before it is too late. Lead indicators often (but not always) relate to the 'soft' issues affecting performance. Managers and the work group will benefit greatly by focusing on lead indicators as well as lag indicators.

Here is a sample of lead performance indicators that might apply to your team. Use this to build your own list of lead performance indicators and review and discuss them every six months with your team. Remember that none of these indicators **alone** guarantees optimum team performance, but the more that they are evident the more likely it is that the desired outcomes will be achieved.

Lead Performance Indicators
- The number of activities initiated to identify the training needs of team members.
- The number of hours staff attend off-the-job training.
- The number of times staff are asked to demonstrate the application of off-the-job training.

- The number of times the reasons staff are attending training are explained and post-training expectations of performance are clarified.
- The number of formal, one-on-one coaching sessions conducted on-the-job per employee.
- The number of staff grievances identified and addressed.
- The number of ideas suggested by staff to improve the way we do things which are implemented.
- The number of non-value adding activities identified and eliminated or modified.
- The number of times the team received formal acknowledgment of good performance.
- The number of incidents of non-compliance with agreed procedures detected.
- The number of workplace hazards identified.
- The number of workplace hazards eliminated or modified .
- The number of safety meetings held.
- The percentage of team members attending safety meetings.
- The percentage of actions implemented from those agreed during team meetings.
- The number of times that team members communication or information requirements are identified.
- The number of times team performance is reviewed.
- The number of activities initiated to remove fear-based perceptions of team members.
- The number of activities initiated to identify and remove 'hidden' blockages to improving team or individual performance.
- The percentage of deliveries from suppliers of raw materials not to specification.
- The number of times each year that performance standards are clarified, agreed and reviewed within the team.
- The number of times that non-performing staff are identified and counselled to improve their performance.
- The number of times we review the effectiveness of our meetings and take action to improve them.
- The number of times that we clarify and agree individual and team priorities.

Tend the garden, pick the flowers

> Growth is the only evidence of life.
> **John Henry Newman**
> *Apologia pro Viat Sua (1864)*
>
> Man is not the sum of what he has already, but rather the sum of what
> he does not have, what he could have.
> **Jean Paul Satre**
> *'Temporalite,' Situations (1947-49),v.1.*

The responsibility for performance management starts and ends with the manager. There is often confusion between performance management and performance appraisal. Because of this there can be suspicion about the motives of the person responsible for managing the performance of staff.

State, up front, the purpose of performance management. Explain that it is about:
- getting staff to be better at their job
- personal and professional growth
- supporting staff in their endeavour to improve
- providing meaningful training and development
- creating a desire for staff to willingly make the improvements needed
- increasing productivity

Here is a step-by-step performance management process you can use.
- Agree the areas in which staff performance will be managed.
- Link these areas to the strategic or team goals of the organisation.
- Identify and document the competencies required in the particular areas
- Discuss and agree the importance of each of these competencies in assisting the staff member to do their job.

- Discuss and agree the extent to which these competencies are currently being performed by the staff member.
- Analyse the perceptions of the manager and the staff member and identify the competencies that both agree are important and not happening as much as they should.
- Select an agreed number of competencies upon which to focus for improvement.
- Discuss the actual meaning of the words that are written down to ensure a common interpretation.
- Agree the actions to take to demonstrate these competencies are being applied.
- Write these actions down on an action plan.
- Check that the staff member is capable of performing the identified competencies, if not:
  - explain what is required there and then; offer another staff member as a mentor or coach; offer specific training related to the specific need.
- Ask the staff member what support they need from you to make the improvement.
- Record all things agreed during the discussion, stating:
  - the what, by whom, by when.
- Inform staff that you will be meeting regularly (every 2 weeks) to review progress and so they can report on the things that were agreed to be done.
- Conduct these meetings every 2 weeks.
- Limit these meetings to 10 minutes per person.
- Ask the staff member to provide verifiable examples of what they have done so far.
- If they have made progress praise them.
- If they have done nothing ask them "What do you intend doing between now and the next meeting?"
- Record anything that is agreed to be done by either you or the staff member.
- Ask them if they are having any problems and provide support where needed.
- Continue with this area of focus until you are both satisfied that the required improvements have been made.
- Select a new area for managing performance and start the process again.

Prevention is better than cure

Every manager has to deal with 'problem' staff. That's why we have managers. It goes with the territory. Avoiding the problem won't make it go away and will seriously undermine your credibility in the eyes of others. Initiating the person's removal to another area can sometimes be a solution if the problem is caused by bad chemistry between the two of you. Usually, however, transferring the 'problem' person to another area is weak management.

Here are some points to consider to prevent or address this situation :

- **Lead by example.** Set the standard. Be a model of the same behaviours expected of staff. Observe company rules, safety standards, etc. and maintain high standards of job performance. Remember that your staff will take their cue from you. They will judge you by what you do not what you say.
- **Act immediately.** Unresolved problems will fester away and erupt more seriously at some point. Many a serious problem could have been prevented if it had been nipped in the bud.
- **Be seen to attempt something positive.** No action on your part will weaken

your effectiveness to manage others. Other staff will wonder why should they comply when so and so gets away with it.

- **Be consistent.** Avoid personal biases. Treat all staff in the same way to prevent being accused of victimisation or favouritism.
- **Clarify expected standards of performance.** Ensure all staff are fully aware of what is expected and your perceptions of how staff are meeting those expectations. Allow staff to take responsibility for setting standards of performance for the team. Discuss and explain changes to policy and procedures before they come into effect.
- **Discipline in private.** Avoid the humiliation and hostility caused by a public dressing down.
- **Act on complaints and grievances immediately.** Regard complaints or grievances as early warnings of worse situations that could follow.
- **Deal with the problem yourself.** Accept that the performance of your staff is your major responsibility. Passing the problem on to another area will be seen as weak management on your part.
- **Keep calm.** If disciplinary action is needed, plan your approach. Gather all the facts about the situation before acting.
- **View it as oppurtunity.** Somebody will be hurting in this situation - consciously or otherwise. This is an opportunity to change something for the better. It can be an opportunity for people to grow and develop.

> "
> When men of talents are punished, authority is strengthened....Every example of punishment has in it some injustice, but the suffering individual is compensated by the public good.
> **Tacitus, c. 55-117**
> *Roman orator, politician, and historian.*
> *Annals of the Julian Emperors.*
> "

Nip it in the bud

> **"** That man (is) far best who can conceive and carry out
> with foresight a wise counsel; next in order (is one) with the sense to
> value and heed such (wise) counsel; while he who can neither initiate it
> (counsel) nor avail himself of it when thrown in his way, is to all intents
> and purposes worthless and good for nothing.
> **Hesiod**
> *Eighth century BC, Greek poet, Works and Days*
>
> Those who do not prevent crimes when they could, encourage them.
> **Cato the Elder, 234 - 149 BC**
> *Roman soldier, statesman, and administrator*
> *Plutarch, The Parallel Lives: Cato the Elder* **"**

One of the least comfortable tasks a manager has to do is to speak to an employee who is being disruptive, producing poor quality work or violating agreed guidelines for behaviour. Most managers do not enjoy this situation and, thus, many shirk it. But bear in mind that it is also highly uncomfortable for the wayward employee. In fact, you can use this discomfort to your advantage.

Simply put, people act to experience pleasant circumstances and act to avoid unpleasant circumstances. You need to make it very clear that both of you have to make certain choices and that each of those choices have consequences - pleasant and unpleasant. Make it clear that one consequence for the employee is that while they continue to misbehave you will continue to counsel them about it. As soon as they improve their behaviour, you will stop counselling them. It's their choice.

Inaction on your part will show you in a poor light in the eyes of other staff. You will be seen as weak and ineffectual and your credibility will suffer. The longer you let it go the worse it will be. Make it easier on yourself by preparing yourself before you actually discuss the problem with the employee - it will really help your confidence.

Answer these questions about the problem situation :
- With whom does it occur and when?
- While talking about what topic or while doing what job?
- Where does the situation occur or where will it recur?
- What specifically does the employee do or say or fail to do or say?
- What specifically do you do or say or fail to do or say?
- What are the consequences if the problem is not resolved?

    Consider :   1. for you
                     2. for the employee
                     3. for the team
                     4. for the customers - both internal and external.

- What outcomes do you desire to resolve this situation?

    Consider :   5. your needs
                     6. their needs
                     7. the team's needs
                     8. the customer's needs - both internal and external.

- What are the possible and probable consequences of speaking up?
- It will help you to actually write down what you will say to this person. Complete these statements :
When you........ When I........ When.......
I would prefer....... I want....... I need....... I would like ....
If you do....... If you do not....... If you will ...... Then I will ....

Invite the person to meet with you in private and tell them that there is a work issue that you need to discuss. Tell them it is something that you need to resolve, but that you can't resolve it without their co-operation. Suggest to them that you will go first and ask them not to interrupt until you have finished. Tell them that they will have their turn and that you will listen to them.

When you have both had your say, begin the process of negotiating an outcome acceptable to both of you. You need to discuss some of the consequences, needs and outcomes previously identified.

Say what?

Okay. So you have a 'problem' employee and you have decided to try to resolve the problem. You've done your preparation (see 'Nip It In The Bud')

Now what do you actually say? Here are some questions and statements to consider. Remember that these are only guidelines and that you will need to adapt them to your situation.

- **Here is a possible opening :**
  "John, there's a situation happening here at work which I need your help on. I'd like to talk it over with you and see if we can find a solution.

  I suggest that I'll describe the situation as I see it and then I'll get your view and then see if we can work something out. I ask you not to interrupt until I finish and I'll do the same for you when it's your turn. Is that fair?

  I'm not here to give you or anybody else a hard time, but I am paid to try to manage this section. I don't like having to do this any more than you probably do, but this situation is affecting others and myself."

- Now using the information from your preparation, describe the situation as you see it. Be specific.
- Describe the consequences of the problem as you see them for all the stakeholders, i.e. all the people who are being affected by this situation.

Here are some other things you might say :
  "John, I can only go by what I see or what I hear. But I may get it wrong. So, rather than jump to conclusions, I would rather talk it over with you and get your view."
  "How do you see the situation?"
  "How do you feel about the situation as I see it?"
  "How do you feel about the consequences as I see them?"
  "Is there anything that I'm doing or not doing that is contributing to this situation?"

"Is there anything that others are doing or not doing that is contributing to this situation?"

"Are there things happening outside work which I don't know about which are contributing to this situation?"

"What do you see as causing this situation?"

"What do you think needs to happen to resolve this?"

"These are the things, as I see them, that are causing the situation...."

"How do you feel about my view? Am I being unfair?"

"What I think needs to happen is this...." (from your preparation, describe what you would like to happen in the future).

"Look, for the reasons I mentioned earlier I need you to :

- do less of this.....(describe the specific improvements)

- do more of this.....

- start doing this....."

"What help do you want from me? What things do you want me to do to help resolve the problem?"

- Agree some actions that both of you will take and set up a time next week to review the situation. Thank John for his time and his contribution.

Something on your mind?

> A man convinced against his will
> is of the same opinion still
> **Abraham Lincoln**

Mindsets - set ways of thinking about things. How many managers would describe themselves as open minded? Possibly most. Yet is anybody really open minded?

All of us carry around in our mind a set of images - our store of life experiences and imaginings. Images about ourselves, our boss, our employees, our colleagues, our customers, the organisation, what's right, what's wrong, what makes sense to us and what doesn't.

These are deeply held beliefs or mindsets which govern our behaviour. Often our mindsets will limit us to comfortable ways of behaving - saying and doing things within our comfort zone. Many of the problems in the workplace are related to the differing perceptions held by the various stakeholders. What we perceive in any given situation is dictated by the images and assumptions which are set in our mind or which we make about the situation.

What we say is often very different from what we are really thinking. But it is what we are really thinking which will dictate our behaviour. Obviously, if what you are really thinking is counter-productive to the situation then keep it to yourself. But be aware that just because a person goes along with what you say, it doesn't necessarily mean that you have their conviction.

If you are attempting to persuade somebody to your point of view so that she or he is genuinely convinced of the course of action which you are proposing, try some of these things:

- Declare your own assumptions about the situation and seek to compare them against the known facts.
- Ask the other person to do the same with any assumptions which they might hold about the situation.
- As the discussion brings out information about the situation, try to separate facts from opinions or inferences.
- Discuss why and where your, and their, assumptions have come from.
- If you have pre-conceived ideas about the situation or the other person(s), state them as notions you hold which you are willing to have challenged.
- Ask the other person(s) to do the same with any pre-conceived ideas that they might hold.
- If it is not counter-productive, tell the other person what you are really thinking and feeling about the situation and let them know that this is really what you think. If you can't do this honestly - don't do it.
- Encourage the other person to tell you what they are really thinking by letting them know that it is important to do this and that you are sincerely interested.
- Let them know that even if what they are really thinking is something unpleasant for you, you would rather know than not know.
- Ask them to describe the consequences of the situation on other stakeholders.
- Ask them to consider whose best interests are being served by the current situation or the proposed situation.
- Ask them why they feel unable to change. Ask them what it is that they are afraid of happening. What is it they are fearful of losing.
- Show them how what you are proposing benefits all stakeholders.
- Discuss with them any negative aspects of your proposal and the consequences on all stakeholders
- Ask them to describe the negative aspects of your proposal from their perspective and then explore with them the reality of these things actually happening.
- Ask them how they feel about things now that we have explored the situation in greater depth.
- Ask them what their level of conviction and commitment is to your proposal.
- Ask them what they will do as a result of this discussion.

Make no enemies

In dealing with cunning persons,
we must ever consider their ends, to interpret their speeches;
and it is good to say little to them,
and that which they least look for.
Francis Bacon, 1561 - 1626
Lord Chancellor of England, Of Negotiating

Forewarned, forearmed; who threats his enemy lends him
a sword to guard himself with.
Louis de Dorfort, c. 1640 - 1709
French-born English statesman and general, Arden of Feversham

Three may keep a secret, if two of them are dead.
Benjamin Franklin, 1706 - 1790
American printer and statesman, Poor Richard's Almanack.

If you are planning a long career in the corporate rat-race, you will need to be adept at corporate or office politics. Don't get me wrong, job performance and learning potential are essential factors in career advancement, but many a bright flame has been extinguished by the murky waters of office politics.

'Politic' is defined in the Australian Concise Oxford Dictionary as (relating to a person) - sagacious, prudent, (of actions, etc.) judicious, expedient; scheming, crafty. If you assume that everybody is honest, forthright and to be trusted, you will, unfortunately, be disappointed. Hopefully, the majority of people you will meet are all these things. Just beware that some people will look you straight in the eye and, with all the sincerity that they can fake, will lie through their teeth. It is nice to be wise after the event - it's even nicer to be wise before the event.

Playing the political game occupies a fair amount of the time of people in bureaucratic organisations in both the private and public sectors. Based on my own experience, however, I'd say that it is rife in the latter.

As politics is a fact of organisational life, you may as well be aware. Here are some things to consider :

- Most people, when push comes to shove, will operate in such a way as to protect or further their own interests. If it is a choice between your interests being served and their personal interests, which choice do you think most people will take?
- Some people have long memories. At the time of an incident where you did not behave according to their expectations, their reaction might be low key, but that incident will be stored away for future use when you have long forgotten it.
- People will not always tell you exactly what they're thinking, but they will convey to you an impression that they are.
- Check around, discretely, and find out the likes and dislikes of senior people within the organisation. Observe them in the workplace and try and gain an idea of their idiosyncrasies. Watch their reaction to the behaviours of other people and mentally note what seems to annoy them and what they seem to favour.
- Find out who are the 'friends' and 'champions' of the bosses and cultivate a relationship with these people.
- Keep your opinions about the performance of higher management to yourself.
- Without being obsequious, take time to acknowledge and thank the personal assistants and secretaries of the bosses.
- Be aware of what you are saying and who you are talking to in social situations or at office or factory functions where you are consuming that old tongue loosener and judgement destroyer - alcohol.
- Think carefully about the message your boss is giving you. Some people don't like to be directive or precise. A vague question or a subtle hint might be their way of saying to you 'this is what I want you to do.'
- Don't contradict or challenge the boss in public unless you are very sure of his or her willingness to let that happen without repercussion.
- Along your travels through the organisational highways, make no enemies.

You stupid bloody idiot!

- USE MISTAKES TO INCREASE AWARENESS

YOU'LL NEVER DO IT, YOU 'ORRIBLE LITTLE OXYGEN THIEF!!

OBSTACLE COURSE

Alston.

That's a very motivating statement isn't it? Guaranteed to encourage a person to improve their performance. Employee surveys confirm that employees rate recognition and praise very highly among things that keep them motivated. Yet surveys continue to reveal that praise and recognition occur far less frequently than employees would prefer.

There are probably several reasons for this. One may be that we tend to take for granted that staff should do a good job anyway - that that's to be expected. It is easy to forget the power of praise. Another reason is that managers are too busy, caught up in their own concerns and lose sight of the need to recognise and praise good performance.

It may be a gender thing - female managers seem to be more comfortable with praising their staff than male managers. Whatever it is, most people respond positively to recognition and praise. The more boring and routine the nature of the work, the more the requirement for recognition and praise.

Here are some guidelines for recognition and praise:
- Establish standards and clearly communicate them so that employees know what good performance looks like. Regularly discuss your expectations

and perceptions of staff performance.

- Keep your ears and eyes open to look for things which merit praise. Look for opportunities to praise and recognise every employee not just your favourites.
- Look for opportunities to praise right efforts as well as right results.
- Consider life from the employee's perspective. What for you might be an easy accomplishment might be quite difficult for the employee.
- Be sincere. Avoid phoney praise. This is unwarranted praise given in the hope that employees will perform well. Provide praise when there is evidence that the employee has performed well or is making improvements.
- Give praise as soon as possible. Immediate recognition is the most effective - left too long, it loses effect.
- Describe in specific terms what the employee did which warrants the praise and how others may be positively affected by their actions.
- Look for opportunities to praise the team as well as individuals.
- Give credit publicly to the team for their achievements.
- Remind yourself constantly that praise is a powerful motivator and that if you make the time to look you will find reason to recognise and praise.

"
Reinforcements continue to be important, of course,
long after an organism has learned how to do something, long after it
has acquired behaviour. They are necessary to maintain
the behaviour in strength.
B.F.Skinner
Harvard University, Harvard Educational Review, 1954.
"

Get the monkeys off your back

How do you respond when a worker brings a problem to your attention which you think they are capable of resolving? Do you hear yourself saying, "OK. Leave it with me. I'll sort it out later?"

In this situation, picture the problem as a monkey on the worker's back. Their intention is to get the monkey off their back and on to your's. Your intention is to get the worker to get rid of the monkey, that is, resolve the problem.

If you are accountable and responsible for resolving the problem, then you deal with it. If the worker is responsible and accountable and has the capability, then send a clear message that you expect them to deal with it.

There is no doubt that some people will attempt to pass the buck up the line. They will keep doing this for as long as the manager lets them.

If your staff are leaving their problems on your desk and you know that they are capable of resolving them, try this approach:

A 'buck passer' will probably say to you, "We've got a problem." At this point, focus on the thought - No. We don't have a problem. You have a problem and that's why we pay you - to solve work problems.

Then ask the worker questions similar to these :
- What is the problem? What are the symptoms of the problem? What are the causes of the problem?
- If they haven't got to the root cause of the problem, keep asking them, "Why do you think that is?" until they get there.
- Who are all the stakeholders? Who are the people who are affected by this problem?
- If we could solve this problem, what would be the ideal outcomes for all key stakeholders?
- What are all the possible things which could be done to solve the problem? What does your intuition tell you to do?
- Don't accept, "I don't know." Prompt them with questions such as these - What might be possible? What could you try? What has worked in the past? What would happen if you were to...?
- Help them to make a list of possible courses of action.
- Ask the worker to consider the consequences of each possible action if it were to be implemented. What would happen if we did this? Will this resolve the problem? How would this affect others? Do we have the resources to do this? Is it really feasible? Will it achieve our outcomes? Will it remove the root cause? Will it create new problems?
- Ask the worker to choose the actions which will provide the best solution. Which actions will resolve the problem with the most positive consequences and the least negative consequences? Will those actions provide the desired outcomes for the stakeholders?
- Agree the sequence of actions to implement.
- Ask the worker to begin implementation and let you know the outcomes or progress made in the following day, week or whatever is appropriate.

Treat the cause, not the symptoms

How many of the solutions managers apply to work and organisational problems fail because the real causes of the problem weren't identified? Thorough analysis of the problem will prevent many headaches later on.

The ideal solution to a problem is one which eliminates the real causes of the problem, i.e. prevents the problem from recurring; is feasible to implement within all constraints (time, money, resources, people, etc.); and by its implementation does not generate other problems.

Analyse a problem by answering these questions:
- What is currently happening that you would like to stop happening?
- What is currently not happening that you would like to happen?
- Who is involved and how are they involved?
- What are the facts about the situation?
- What are the assumptions and inferences about the situation?
- What forces are operating to maintain the situation?
- What things could be happening which are not obvious that could be causing the problem?
- How could we think about the causes in different ways?
- What thought processes or perspectives could be preventing us from seeing the real causes? What do we see if we change those thought processes or perspectives?
- When does the problem happen? Under what conditions?
- How often does the problem happen?
- How does the problem happen?
- Where does the problem happen? In particular locations?
- What are the symptoms of the problem? Why does each one occur? (Use what is referred to as 'repetitive why analysis' - ask 'why' five times or until you can no longer come up with a new reason).
- Is the problem caused by systems and procedures or by people's behaviour?

- Are you looking at the causes or the effects?
- Are the causes visible or invisible?
- Is the problem isolated or spread over a number of areas?
- What things have changed within the environment in which the problem is located?
- Is the problem there all the time or does it come and go?
- Is the problem due to too much of something or too little of something?
- How is the problem connected with other happenings?
- What would be happening if the problem didn't exist?

If a man begins with certainties, he shall end in doubts;
but if he will be content to begin with doubts,
he shall end in certainties.
Francis Bacon, 1561-1626.
Lord Chancellor of England, Advancement of Learning.

Discovery (of a solution) consists of looking at the same thing as
everyone else and thinking something different.
Albert Szent-Gyorgyi
*Nobel laureate in medicine and physiology, Ouch, A Whack on the Side of the
Head, (Warner,1983)*

The correct solution to any problem depends principally on a true
understanding of what the problem is.
Arthur Mellen Wellington, 1847-1895.
*Civil engineer and pioneer Operations Research scientist.
The Economic Theory of Railway Location, 1887.*

A project manager's checklist

As a manager you will occasionally be asked to join a project team or to lead a project team. This checklist identifies a range of actions which will help ensure a successful project outcome.

- Gather and analyse the facts regarding the current situation - the status of the project.
- Define or re-define the problem - identifying the core issues and causes.
- Set project objectives and outcomes.
- Develop performance indicators or standards for successful completion of the project.
- Develop possible strategies.
- Identify the negative consequences of each strategy.
- Decide on a basic strategy.
- Identify the stakeholders (anybody who can influence the successful outcomes of the project) and what is required from each stakeholder - a decision, information or action.
- Brainstorm a list of project activities, tasks and functions.
- Decide priorities, sequence and time requirements for each activity.
- Develop key performance indicators for major activities.
- Decide who in the project team will do what, provide what or obtain what.
- Determine the requirement for resources including budget, equipment, facilities, etc.
- Prepare requests for proposals - consultants, contractors, suppliers, etc.
- Review, evaluate, negotiate and finalise tenders.
- Assign responsibility, accountability and authority to project team members so they can carry out their activities.
- Identify and explore areas of high risk and uncertainty
- Identify strategic control points - activities or events or things for which serious setbacks can be suffered if problems are not detected and prevented.
- Establish preventative and corrective measures. If....., then.....
- Define areas of intra and interdepartmental co-operation - what is the nature of the co-operation? What specifically is required?
- Prepare support documents - policy manuals, procedures, research material, etc.

- Plan meeting dates and times.
- Prepare a document (project action plan) which includes all the necessary information including a schedule of project activities for each project team member.
- Select and train other project personnel (as needed).
- Disseminate policy, procedural documents, and information about the project to all relevant stockholders.
- Conduct project activities, tasks and functions.
- Monitor the performance of major activities.
- Monitor the performance of people on the project team - evaluate the effectiveness of the team.
- Exercise project control activities - corrective actions in response to deviations from standards.
- Evaluate the actual project outcomes against the stated outcomes.
- Write a final report.
- Implement plans for the transfer of responsibility to the client or user.
- Follow up in relation to the outcome of the project.
- Communicate the results of the project to all stakeholders.
- Acknowledge and thank all project team members and other contributing people.

As ye sow so shall ye reap

PERSONAL APPEARANCE AND IMPACT ON THE AUDIENCE.....

HELL'S ANGELS RALLY

Unfortunately - if you are looking for shortcuts - when it comes to public speaking, there is no substitute for preparation. Prepare well - present well. Prepare poorly - present poorly.

All honest managers admit to a degree of nerves or anxiety at the thought of public speaking. Just a quick thought here - it is not 'public speaking' per se that makes you nervous. It is the images you have created in your mind about yourself and public speaking that produces your anxiety. And anyway, a degree of anxiety is necessary as it is the signal that you are gearing up to perform well.

Back to preparation. Here are some things to consider when preparing for public speaking:
- Clarify what the subject is.
- Think about how the subject relates to the audience. What is it that the audience

will be expected to do with the information? What is the audience likely to know about the subject?

- Be there 10 minutes before you are due to commence. Know how long you will be speaking for.
- Check out the venue to determine how to make best use of the room layout and existing aids and equipment.
- Decide how to address the group - standing or sitting in front, using a lectern or public address system, or sitting in as part of the group.
- Develop a plan which includes how to introduce the subject, what topics of the subject will be covered and key points to be made about each topic. Also include points to be summarised and emphasised at the end of the presentation.

Some pointers about delivering your speech or presentation:
- Arrive early to ensure the layout is right and all the resources are available and working.
- Check your personal appearance. Be aware of the impact your clothes will have on the audience.
- Speak with conviction and confidence about the subject matter - gained through your thorough preparation. Never make apologies for the subject matter.
- Use a natural delivery and speak at the right volume, pace and tone to suit the situation. Remember to vary your tone.
- Speak to all in the group. Look at all people at various times during your speech. Avoid the temptation to address only one or two. Don't gaze at the roof or the back wall or through a window.
- Be alive - use appropriate emotion, energy and movement, but avoid pacing back and forth continuously.
- Anticipate questions that may arise. If unable to answer a question at the time, make a note of it and get back to the person later.
- If reading from prepared material, look up frequently at the audience.
- Summarise the main points of the speech.

Free sex

Now that I have the undivided attention of some of you, I'll get to the point of this article - presentations or public speaking. This is one activity that strikes fear into the heart of most managers. To reduce your anxiety and to ensure a successful presentation, focus on one thought - preparation, preparation, and more preparation.

The first few moments of a presentation can make it or break it. It will help you set up your presentation or speech if you can kick it off with a powerful introduction. How you perform in the first few minutes is very important because it is then when your audience is forming their impressions of you and what you are about to present. Get them 'on side' at the beginning and you are half way home.

Use this acronym **INTRO** to help put your introduction together.

I interest
How do you intend to capture the audience's attention with something that is relevant to the subject? The solution may be a joke, anecdote, question, compliment, shock, startling fact, a provocative or controversial comment or a curiosity.

N need
Your introduction should explain why the audience needs to listen. In what way will the audience gain or benefit from the information you're about to give them? What will be different for them as a result of listening to your presentation? If you are struggling to explain why people need to listen to your presentation - forget it.

T title
What are you going to call your presentation? For example, would you title your presentation 'Public Speaking' or 'How to overcome nerves and enjoy public speaking'? The latter is likely to gain more attention.

R range
This has two elements - the range of topics you intend to cover in the time allotted and how long you intend to take to cover the range from beginning to end.

Remember that as you announce a time frame, the audience sets its mental alarm which may bring on a mental walkout if the timeframe is exceeded.

O   objective

What is it that you want the audience to do as a result of listening to your presentation? What is the specific action you would like them to take after your presentation? What results do you wish to accomplish?

Good luck. Now all you need is an equally powerful body of content and an equally powerful ending.

CAPTURE THE AUDIENCE'S ATTENTION...

Very interesting....

So you have to make a public presentation? How do you kick it off in a high energy way which immediately focuses the audience's attention? Try some of these ideas.

- Show a bright, colourful visual or make a loud noise. For example, a gory picture of an eye operation makes an enormous impact at the start of a safety talk.
- Create curiosity. Ever wondered how...? Ever wondered when ... ? Ever wondered what...? Ever wondered why...?
- Pay a sincere compliment to the group or to an individual. Make sure the compliment is genuine and relevant. Describe why it is worthy of mention.
- State a significant consequence of an upcoming event or state a fact of interest to the group. For example, "Ignorance of this particular law in the future makes you liable to a fine of $25,000 and/or imprisonment for a term of 6 months."
- Ask a question. This will gain immediate audience response and hence their immediate attention. "We are here today to find out more about_____. Does anyone know why _____ is of vital interest to this group?"

- Ask a series of questions around Rudyard Kipling's six wise men - who, what, where, how, why and when.
- State a benefit for the audience. Tell the audience what's in it for them, how they will benefit by listening to your presentation. It might be more profit, reduced costs, time saving, more leisure time, increased efficiency, less stress, better safety, etc.
- Display a model directly related to your subject - an ingenious cutaway model or transparent perspex dummy can be shown to reveal parts related to your subject.
- Start with a 'straw poll' of the audience. Ask the audience to put up their hand if they are for proposition X or Y or Z.
- In advance of the presentation, conduct a mini survey on the topic and then present the findings.
- Promise things to come - some interesting development or result or reward without disclosing exactly what it is.
- Quote a recommendation or referral which has come from someone well known and respected by the audience - mention that person's name and why they have recommended you.
- Start with a personalised statement connecting you immediately with the topic. "I lost 10 years of my life using heroin and like you I thought it would never happen to me."
- Show the end result first. This is what you will know or be able to do as a result of this presentation.
- Tell a joke or cite an humorous incident about the topic. Check with others first that it is funny and you can tell it humorously.
- Use a startling statistic. Relate it to something which occurs in everyday life to sheet it home.
- Ask the audience to tell you what are the burning questions or issues of most interest to them relating to the topic.

Read and digest

> A man ought to read just as inclination leads him,
> for what he reads as a task will do him little good.
> **Samuel Johnson**
> *Quoted in Boswell's Life of Samuel Johnson, July 14, 1763.*
>
> What is reading but silent conversation.
> **Walter Savage Landor**
> *'Aristoteles and Callisthenes,'*
> *Imaginary Conversations (1824 - 53)*

Did you know that the average adult reads to the ability level of a 12 year old? To succeed as a manager we need to be better than the average. More importantly, it means that there are some skills required for effective reading that some managers do not possess.

How do we balance the need to gain full meaning of what we are reading with the need to limit the time we actually spend reading?

To state the obvious, reading is an important skill for managers to have. You need to be able to read quickly and to get to the heart of the matter without having to wade through reams and reams of text. Skimming and scanning are ways to do this that will enable you to focus on the content without having to read every word.

There are many types of speed reading courses that train you to glean information quickly. Much of the methodology relies on some simple skills and the reader practising and developing those skills.

In no particular order, try these to help you read for a quick understanding of content.

- Remove any external distractions before you start to read.
- Read through the contents page before tackling the article, document or book - this will give you an overview of what it contains.
- Identify topics that relate to things you need to know about at that moment.
- Read any summary that may exist before reading anything else, e.g. the executive summary - this will provide you with a context for the rest of the text.
- Read the first and last chapter of the document / book.
- Read the first and last paragraph of every chapter.
- Read the first sentence of every paragraph.
- Look at the chapter headings or document title and brainstorm in your mind what you know about this topic before you start reading.
- Identify key words which are relevant and current to the information you want. Then read from the top and bottom of a page and locate these words.
- Use a high-lighter to help you locate clusters of key words - if there are a lot in one area then read all the surrounding text.
- Locate words with which you are unfamiliar - jargon, acronyms or unknown. Then find out the meanings of these words before starting the overall task.
- Read the sentence before the one containing the words, the sentence containing the words and the sentence after the one containing the words.
- Use the index to locate key topics or text about which you may wish to find information.
- Read any glossary of terms that may exist.
- Make notes about key points for later reference.
- Mark (underline or circle) the important text so you can refer to it quickly at a later date.
- Discuss with other people, who have read the same text, their interpretations, understandings, impressions, thoughts, evaluations and opinions of what the content was about.
- Re-read the text where it has not made sense to you.

Knowledge is power

How do managers keep up to date with all the required reading that crosses their desk? If you are like most managers the answer is - with great difficulty. Yet you need to keep your knowledge base 'topped up'. Ever thought about planning how you read?

Most of us probably read in an ad hoc, reactive manner. There are benefits in taking a more planned, proactive approach to reading. You plan your recreational activities, you plan your holidays, you plan your family life, you plan your work day, etc. so why not plan your reading, i.e. the what, how and when you read.

It is fair to say that some of the things you have to read are outside your control, but most of what you read is within your control.

Here are some tips on proactive reading without loss of comprehension. (Check your motive for improving your reading practices. If you have none, then read something else).
- Sort your reading into two piles - recreational reading and business reading. (Here we are mainly focusing on business reading - books, magazines, news papers, periodicals, journals, etc. related to your business.)
- Sort your business reading into four piles. (1) - must read, (2) - should read, (3) could read, (4) - never read.
- Next, take the material in pile (3) and place it in pile (1), (2) or (4).
- Now take the material in pile number (4) and place in your rubbish or re-cycling bin. You'll enjoy that.
- As new material comes your way, immediately assign it to pile (1), (2) or the bin.
- Allocate a set time during your day or night for business reading and put it in your diary or use your lunch break. Organise others so that you won't be disturbed during your allocated reading time.
- Read books, magazines, journals, etc. the same way you read a newspaper. Start a book at the beginning, but scan each chapter only reading headings or sub-headings which are of interest to you or which you need to read.
- Before you read a book, for example, decide some questions to ask of the book.

Write them down - make a list. If the topic is completely unknown to you, scan the list of contents and the subject index and then develop your list of questions.

- Start with your most important question and using the list of contents or subject index read only those pages of the book which deal directly with your question.
- Then choose the next most important question and repeat the process.
- Scan the relevant chapter for key words or phrases which relate to your questions.
- Go to the end of the chapter and read the summary of that chapter and only read the chapter if it interests you or you need to.
- When reading a page, decide what key words or phrases you are looking for before you begin. Using your finger to focus your eyes, move your finger from left to right going down the page only stopping when you find the key words or phrases you are looking for.

Ask me no questions and I'll tell you no lies

> If you ask people confidentially what they want
> most in their job - if they're paid anything decent at all - they will say
> that they want a greater sense of self worth.... And I think this giving of
> responsibility and respect and authority is one of the
> things that motivates people.
> **Fritz Maytag**
> *President, Anchor Brewing Co, Harvard Business Review*
>
> There's no telling how far a person can go if he's willing to
> let other people take the credit.
> **Robert Woodruff**
> *Chief Executive Officer, Coca Cola Inc. Magazine, August 1987*

A manager was once asked, "How do you know if you are doing a good job?" His response was, "If I'm not getting a kick in the pants then things must be okay." Unfortunately, the only time some workers get any feedback on their performance is when something goes wrong. This is an example of negative reinforcement. That's probably not the intention of most managers, but that's how it comes across to the worker.

A business owner each year distributed a Christmas bonus to his work force. This caused complaints from some of his people because they got less than others. When they complained to him, he explained why. With each complainant, he went through a list of the things that they had done during the year which were examples of poor job performance or examples of low commitment or co-operation. **Now** they learned what the criteria were for getting the better bonuses.

People thrive on recognition and acknowledgment. We all know that, but we seem to take for granted the good performance of our workers and forget to acknowledge their efforts regularly. "Thank you. You do a great job" delivered sincerely and when deserved costs you no time or effort, but has a powerful impact.

An employee of a client once told me that she would welcome feedback on her job performance from her manager. And she stressed not just what she was doing well, but what she was doing that was seen to be unsatisfactory.

Recognition and feedback are important to maintaining and improving individual performance. Here are some things to do:

- Identify the expectations and perceptions of staff concerning the degree of recognition and feedback they receive. Ask them. It might be uncomfortable for you and them, but - no pain, no gain.
- Ask staff to suggest ways to provide recognition and feedback.
- Conduct regular 'recognition and feedback' meetings.
- Look for opportunities to acknowledge the good performance of staff.
- Identify the aspects of their job that each person does well.
- Identify the aspects of their job that each person could improve.
- Provide each person with regular feedback covering things done well and things to improve.
- Acknowledge 'right efforts' as much as 'right results'.
- Seek regular feedback on your own performance. To make this easier on both parties ask them to tell you things they would like you to do more of and to do less of.
- Make provision for rewards and recognition to be given.
- Praise in public, provide constructive criticism in private.
- Direct feedback toward behaviour that the other person can do something about.
- Describe the actual behaviour rather than evaluating it when giving feedback on performance.
- Maintain a balance between positive and negative feedback
- Check to see the message about future expectations was received as intended.
- Give feedback about the particular behaviour to be addressed at the earliest opportunity.
- Discuss and agree standards of performance.
- Ensure that your expectations of each person are clear and accepted.

Damned with faint praise

When you conduct a survey of staff to identify things they would like to see improved related to how they are managed, recognition and feedback always ranks high on their list.

Here are some ways to improve recognition and feedback :

HOW TO PRAISE
- Give your praise as soon as possible after the event.
- Make it personal - use the employee's name.
- Be specific and objective about what you are praising.
- Explain why their performance is important to you, to themselves and to the company.
- Be positive and sincere in manner and tone of voice.
- Don't give with one hand and take away with the other by asking for an even bigger and better effort next time.
- Make it short and sweet and don't embarrass them.

WHAT TO PRAISE
- Give appropriate praise to employees for :
  a) outstanding performance
  b) consistently good performance
  c) standard performance when usual performance is below standard
  d) improvement in performance following counselling
  e) right efforts even if the right results aren't there just yet.
- Know what your people are doing so that you know when to praise.

HOW TO GIVE CONSTRUCTIVE CRITICISM
- Maintain self esteem. Separate the aspect of their behaviour from them as a whole person.
- Focus on the behaviour rather than the person.
- Use a counselling approach.
- Do it in private.
- Do it as soon as possible after the event.

- Review one problem at a time.
- Give credit for what is being done right.
- Be specific and objective about what concerns you.
- Agree the facts.
- Discuss the reasons.
- Look for solutions together.
- Agree on an action plan for both of you.
- Show your confidence in the employee.
- Leave the door open for further discussion.

Never trust a skinny cook

Without feelings of respect,
what is there to distinguish men from beasts?
Confucius
Analects (6th c. B.C.), 2.7, tr. Ch'u Chai and Winberg Chai

We can always make ourselves liked provided we are likeable,
but we cannot always make ourselves esteemed,
no matter what our merits are.
Nicolas Malebranche
Trait de la morale (1867)

Why are some people more respected than others? What do they do that sets them apart? Two of the qualities they possess are a greater awareness of where they fit into the big picture and an awareness about themselves as individuals. They have no pretences.

We can respect people for the many individual qualities they possess be it their determination, intelligence or just plain kindness. To be respected as a whole person is the ultimate and reflects a combination of special qualities. How well do you measure up in this department?

- Seek feedback from staff members as to what their perceptions are about an issue. Ask them what they are thinking and how they are feeling about it.
- Actively listen to what people are telling you and demonstrate that you have listened by paraphrasing what they have said.
- Demonstrate an interest in their culture by asking them to present a point of view from their perspective.
- Present your point of view in an objective and factual manner by avoiding

190

making value judgements and providing verifiable evidence where possible.

- Demonstrate a sense of humour by laughing along with the group or being involved in the odd, harmless, office antic. Beware of not to going too far.
- Show that you can laugh at yourself if and when a situation arises.
- Respect the confidentiality of staff members where sensitive issues are involved by ensuring they are counselled or disciplined in private.
- Avoid losing your temper, being sarcastic, being cynical or showing your frustration where it will damage your image, the image of someone else or the image of the organisation.
- Demonstrate fairness and consistency when making judgements and decisions.
- Demonstrate honesty.
- Avoid embarrassing staff members in front of their peers.
- Ask staff how they would like to be recognised for outstanding work. Some public praise can cause embarrassment.
- Model the behaviours you wish the staff members to exhibit.
- Do what you say you are going to do.
- Know the technical requirements of the jobs you are managing.
- Demonstrate loyalty to the organisation by speaking positively about it and the staff.
- Recognise and reward staff members who demonstrate the behaviours the organisation is trying to engender.
- Provide support to staff who are endeavouring to comply with the requests of the organisation. This may be in the form of either resources or encouragement.
- Treat all people equally regardless of status.
- Admit it when you are wrong and apologise to the other person.
- Be prepared to admit your own short comings.
- Give credit where it is due - don't pass off team member's efforts or ideas as your own.

Don't look at me...

> A strong sense of identity gives man an idea
> he can do no wrong; too little accomplishes the same.
> **Djuna Barnes**
> *Nightwood (1937)*
>
> Rose is a rose is a rose is a rose.
> **Gertrude Stein**
> *'Sacred Emily,' Geography and Plays (1922)*

How often do we hear "that's not my job" or "I didn't know I was supposed to do that" or "whose job is it?" This confusion, more often than not, is a result of a lack of clarification of roles.

Life at work can be far less confusing if we know:

- who should be doing what and
- what our responsibilities are

Clarification of responsibilities is a management function and is best done in consultation with the team members.

Having roles clearly defined and accepted will lessen the time to do things, reduce conflict, reduce duplication of effort, increase productivity and reduce stress.

- Discuss with staff the benefits of having their and your roles clearly defined.
- Discuss with staff their role.
- Ask them what they think it is and confirm what it should be. Where necessary,

give a clear description of what you believe their job is.

- Discuss your role with staff.

- Ask them what they think your role should be. Where necessary, give them a clear description of what your job is.

- Describe the tasks and functions that need to be performed by the positions in question.

- Discuss the standards and your expectations of the position.

- Allocate tasks in an equitable manner to ensure that one person isn't doing an unfair work load. Involve staff in the work allocation exercise.

- Determine the level of authority for each position and ensure all are fully aware of these limits.

- Inform others of the authority level which comes with the position.

- Discuss with staff, with like job functions, what tasks each will perform and to what standard.

- Agree who performs the function, who is consulted, who is advised of the result, who provides the information and who makes the decision.

- Document the role for each position and provide all staff with a copy. Get them to read it and then sign it to say they have read and understood it.

- Inform all team members of the role of other positions.

- Review roles on an ongoing basis. Do this each time a new staff member is appointed to the area, new jobs are allocated to the area, staff leave, staff take leave, restructuring occurs, new strategic plans are developed or every 12 months as a minimum.

- Discuss with the staff member concerned the importance of the role being carried out to the agreed standard.

- Help the staff member to perform their role by checking that they have the required resources, support, knowledge, skills and motivation.

Where does that buck stop?

A 'role matrix' or 'accountability matrix' is a very useful tool for clarifying the roles, responsibilities and accountabilities of your work group or team. It is simple to construct and makes it much easier for the individuals to see who does what. A manager can do this alone and then discuss it with the team or prepare it together with the team.

This is how to construct your 'role matrix':
- Take a sheet of blank paper - size A3 or A4.
- Down the left hand side of the page (the long side), make a list of all the key activities or functions which are performed by the team. (Not the 6-9 key result areas, but the key activities related to each key result area. You could have between 20 to 50. The more you have, the more role clarification you will achieve.)
- The activities do not need to be listed in sequence.
- Try to keep your matrix to one page (which is why A3 may be better), but if necessary go to two.
- For each activity you have listed, draw a line right across the page.
- Write the initials of each team member including yourself across the top of the page from left to right.
- Draw a column for each person from top to bottom. You now have your blank matrix or grid.
- Leave a narrow space at the bottom of the page for the following code (or develop a code that better suits you):

  CODE   P - Performs action   C - is Consulted for opinion

                I - provides factual Information   O - is informed of Outcomes

                D - makes the Decision   X - not involved in any way
- Start with the first activity and consider the first team member listed across the top.
- Allocate a code letter or letters which best describe that person's role in relation to the activity and write the letter(s) in the empty box.
- For example, if that person's role is to actually carry out that activity then allocate a 'P'. If that person performs the task, is consulted for their opinion and is informed of the progress, then allocate 'PCO'.

- Repeat this process for each other team member for that activity.
- Repeat the entire process for each activity until each team member's role has been described.
- Discuss the 'role matrix' with your team and issue a copy to each person.
- Review on a yearly basis or as the roles and functions of your team change.

Responsibility And Accountability Grid

CODES		
	P	**P**erforms Action
	I	Provides Factual **I**nformation & / or Resources
	C	Is **C**onsulted Re Opinion
	A	Is **A**dvised of Action / Outcome
	D	Makes **D**ecision
	X	Not Involved in Any Way

TEAM MEMBERS

ACTIVITIES FUNCTIONS PROCESSES

Back to front

> The superior man encourages people to approach him,
> by his readiness to receive them.
> **I Change : Book of Changes**
> *China, c. 600 BC*
>
> To lead the people, walk behind them.
> **Lao-Tzu, c. 604-c. 531 BC**
> *Chinese philosopher and founder of Taoism, Tao Te Change.*
>
> Use your own best judgement at all times.
> **Nordstrom Corp**
> *Entire contents of $1.9 billion company's Policy Manual.*

Yesterday's supervisor is today's frontline manager. Is this just a new word to describe the same role? Not quite. Today's supervisor - frontline manager - has a broader role than she or he had in the past. It is probably a sign of the devolution of management authority and decision making down to lower levels in the organisation. This has come about as the realisation spreads that the people closer to the 'coalface' are better placed to handle some of the traditional management functions previously reserved for managers higher up the corporate tree.

So what are the functions of frontline managers? Here is a checklist of the role and functions of the frontline manager. Many of these functions are best done in partnership with team members.

- Establishing work goals and standards of performance for team members.
- Planning work allocation and identifying priorities.
- Planning work organisation.

- Planning staff requirements for particular jobs.
- Clarifying work roles and functions.
- Organising and co-ordinating the work of staff.
- Assessing staff training needs.
- Creating an environment where staff are able to learn from each other.
- Conducting on-the-job training and coaching.
- Initiating off-the-job training activities and actively supporting and managing the application of new skills in the workplace.
- Identifying and supplying staff and management requirements for information.
- Applying safe working practices.
- Identifying and dealing with staff complaints and grievances.
- Providing recognition and feedback to staff.
- Developing teamwork.
- Providing direction and support to the team.
- Monitoring staff performance.
- Counselling and disciplining problem employees.
- Identifying and dealing with workplace conflict.
- Reviewing the way we work as a team.
- Consulting with staff to identify and resolve work related problems.
- Identifying the problems, needs and concerns of the work group.
- Communicating the problems and concerns of staff to management.
- Incorporating the ideas and suggestions of staff to continuously improve systems and procedures and work practices.
- Communicating the ideas and suggestions of staff to higher management and policy and system designers.
- Identifying causes of low morale or low motivation and acting to address them.
- Facilitating the implementation of change.
- Improving the quality of products and services to internal and external customers.
- Managing team performance to achieve goals and outcomes.

Think safety first, second and third!

> Not a gift of a cow, nor gift of land,
> nor yet a gift of food, is so important as the gift of safety,
> which is declared to be the great gift among all gifts in this world.
> **Panchatantra**
> *(c. 5th c.), 1, tr. Franklin Edgerton*

Over the past decade, safety has become a huge issue in the workplace and is continuing to have a huge impact on the way the work is and will be done. Management has a 'Duty of Care' to ensure the work environment is safe for everyone.

Part of the dilemma for management is the cost to address many of the 'safety issues' which have been identified. Many of these issues have been around for a long time, but have never been considered important. The emphasis of responsibility, however, has shifted from the individual (to take care) to the organisation (to make it safe.)

Both litigation and legislation are acting as powerful incentives for organisations to ensure that the worksite is safe. By applying these actions you will meet most of the criteria for a safe work environment.

- Appoint a safety officer who can assume the role of 'watch dog'.
- Establish a safety committee, comprising staff and management to oversee key safety issues and make decisions.
- Identify and highlight hazards and areas which are unsafe.
- Determine the cause of hazards and act immediately to rectify the situation.
- Implement action immediately to restrict use of unsafe areas or things and to limit danger.

- Establish a procedure for dealing with unsafe situations and equipment.
- Establish clear criteria by which objective and rational assessment can be made.
- Inform staff of any safety concern you may have as soon as is practical. Make sure you get a response from them so that you know they have received the warning.
- Notify the appropriate authority to deal with the hazard where it is beyond the skills of you or staff, e.g. electrical, chemical or structural problems.
- Establish and document an organisation evacuation procedure.
- Ensure all areas display, in a prominent place, a copy of the evacuation procedure.
- Practise and update evacuation procedures regularly.
- Discuss with staff the implications of 'Duty of Care' and what their role might be in this area.
- Include specific organisation safety issues into the organisation induction program.
- Ensure equipment complies with national safety standards before purchasing it for the organisation.
- Budget for the replacement of equipment which may be becoming unsafe.
- Reward and recognise people who are safety conscious.
- Provide regular safety training courses for staff and committee members which relate specifically to workplace safety.
- Learn about the legislative requirements of management in relation to occupational health and safety. Do this by reading literature, attending courses, inviting government safety representatives to the worksite to talk to staff and conduct safety audits.

Safety is no accident, you have to prepare for it

Accident is defined as an event that is without apparent cause or unexpected; an unlucky event, especially one causing injury or damage. (The Australian Concise Oxford Dictionary). "Unlucky" will undoubtedly console the family of a worker killed in the workplace and explain the reasons their father or brother or sister had to die. (There are not too many managers killed in the workplace.)

The term 'accident' is an unfortunate one as it conveys an acceptance of the unnecessary. 'We're terribly sorry you have lost an eye, but it was only an accident.' As if 'accident' excuses the maiming for life or the death. No one need be killed or injured at work and when they are, there is always a reason. Always.

Unintentional happenings are also described as accidents. So what is your intention when you deliberately choose not to replace unsafe equipment or deliberately choose not to follow a safety procedure? Is it to take a chance with somebody else's life or even your own?

Here is a checklist for managers who believe that death and injury in the workplace are preventable.
- Identify the requirements for safety training.
- Check where safety rates as a priority in the minds and actions of you and your work group. What is the safety culture like within your team?

- Discuss the attitudes within the team towards safety, accidents, death and injury.
- Ensure regular, 'hands on' safety training of all team members.
- Evaluate the effectiveness of the training in terms of what people think and do in relation to safety, i.e. check that people are applying the safety training in the workplace.
- Keep safety as a constant focus in the minds of your work group.
- Conduct regular 'toolbox' safety training.
- Ensure all hazardous areas and equipment are clearly marked.
- Ensure safe operating procedures are clearly visible and followed.
- Encourage your people to report anything to you which they perceive to be unsafe. Ensure that workers believe that they can report concerns without fear of consequences.
- Check what pressure is placed on people to ignore safe limits and safe practices.
- Ensure all new operators undergo safety training before commencing work.
- Check that all staff are informed of and understand safety procedures.
- Instil an attitude within your team that accidents don't just happen, that there is always a reason and that all accidents are preventable if we are focussed and aware.
- Check that all legislative and company safety requirements are met on site.
- Act immediately on unsafe practices - never tolerate non-compliance with safe working practices.
- Regularly check potential safety hazards.
- Act on workers' complaints and concerns immediately or as soon as possible. Otherwise they won't bother.
- Encourage workers to take responsibility for the safety of themselves and their own workmates.
- Remind workers that not one casualty believed that they would be injured or killed that day.
- Investigate incidents to establish causes and implement the necessary changes.
- Conduct regular safety audits to identify safety hazards and unsafe practices.

Accentuate the positives.
Eliminate the negatives.

Reinforcement is a powerful management tool. A manager needs to consider what she says and does by way of reinforcement for individual and team performance. The most important consideration being how the actions of the manager are perceived by staff. It is staff who decide whether your actions are seen by them as positive reinforcement or negative reinforcement.

It is generally accepted that people respond better to positive reinforcement than to negative reinforcement. Yet employees will generally tell you they get far more negative feedback (reinforcement) than positive feedback.

If you manage a team who are required to promote and sell your products and services, here are a number of things to say and do to keep them achieving sales targets.

- Recognise and reward the successes and discuss the effect on our customers and on our business.
- Make feedback on efforts and results immediate.
- Provide weekly feedback on the team's progress toward team goals.
- Acknowledge and reinforce movement towards the achievement of sales goals - acknowledge 'small step' improvement.
- Look for opportunities to observe examples of people doing the right things - and discuss these with the team.
- Identify areas of weakness and provide coaching or mentoring.
- Ask your team to suggest ways to provide reinforcement.
- Reinforce the importance of the intrinsic reward that goes with accomplishment.
- Determine needs, feedback and information requirements, and the nature of assistance they require on a regular basis.
- Encourage staff to stretch themselves by renegotiating slightly higher sales targets.
- Recognise individual differences in capabilities and negotiate individual sales targets accordingly.

- Clarify and discuss the actions to perform which will most likely lead to sales.
- Discuss peoples' attitudes to selling and link those attitudes to behaviours.
- Identify and discuss the impact on behaviour of mental blockages to selling.
- Use mistakes as opportunities to increase awareness and develop new skills.
- Keep staff informed of the 'big picture' results.
- Encourage your best people to discuss their approach within the team.
- Ask for new ideas at every sales team meeting.
- Identify typical problems or objections to overcome and discuss within the team things to do and say to overcome them.
- Ensure individual achievement gains recognition at higher levels.
- Share success stories always identifying the learnings to be gained.
- Acknowledge 'right efforts' as much as 'right results'.

If I.... would you...?

Sales managers can use this checklist with their sales team to improve their negotiating skills when selling.

- Spend time preparing before you negotiate a sale - plan first, negotiate second.
- Prepare from the client's perspective - identify the important issues for the client.
- During negotiation, listen without interruption.
- Use silence as a tactic - let the buyer break the silence.
- Know exactly what it is that you are prepared to concede.
- Look for changes in body language to indicate the level of receptivity of the buyer.
- Find their best position before giving away any concessions.
- Summarise and prioritise the client's needs.
- Be aware of your initial instinctive response - it may work better to hold off

until you have more information.
- Avoid making desperate decisions - remember that you have something they need or want.
- Use 'if.... then....' questions. If I do this.... then would you do....?
- Avoid presenting your best deal first.
- If your first attempt is unsuccessful, have a fall back position prepared.
- Avoid jargon or negative terms.
- Present what you're proposing as a partnership - how can we work together to get what we both want?
- Clarify their objections to check that you are getting to their real objections.
- Allow the client some concessions.
- Avoid rushing negotiations. Rushing the client will make them uncomfortable and uncomfortable people tend to not make buying decisions.
- Obtain commitments along the way during the negotiations.
- Ask how you can reasonably assist the customer.
- Be willing to share information to demonstrate openness and trust.
- Know your own limits - don't exceed them.
- Show that you are looking for a win/win outcome.
- Anticipate objections and have prepared responses.
- Avoid making promises that we can't deliver.
- Explore every possible benefit for the client of your proposal or product.
- Use a non-aggressive tone of voice - be friendly.
- Explore all options available.
- Avoid criticising competitors - show why our product is different and better.
- Avoid information overload - too much information will confuse. Provide chunks of information as appropriate.
- Avoid making the first concession.
- Trade concessions for concessions.
- Ask if your deal or proposition is fair?
- Get an 'agree to agree' agreement up front - let's agree to work towards agreement rather than towards a stand off.
- Allow time. Avoid negotiating close to a deadline - you don't need the pressure unless you can use it to your advantage.

Managing sales performance 1

Many organisations which traditionally have been reactive sales and service providers have been forced through increased competition and changing customer expectations to change to a proactive sales and service culture. Managers have to manage this process and establish a performance management process. This will work better if it is a two-way process, i.e. the team member has input in the performance management process.

CLARIFY PURPOSE
- Explain why the organisation is asking for changes and moving into a more proactive sales and service culture.
- Discuss the budget and product targets for the organisation as a whole and our team in particular.

EXPLAIN EXPECTATIONS
- Ask team members to ask questions and to discuss their thoughts and feelings about what is happening.
- Explain the results expected of them and of others in the organisation.
- Explain the key sales and sales management actions for you and them.
- Define your role as trainer/coach, facilitator and sales manager in the sales and service culture.
- Discuss the specific, sales performance indicators, i.e. clarify how you will be assessing the implementation of the new and different ways of proactive sales and service.
- Negotiate sales behaviour or action goals including the frequencies of the actions, e.g. daily, weekly, monthly.
- Negotiate financial goals and/or product volume goals.

MONITOR PROGRESS
- Discuss how you will:
  - review efforts and results with them individually on a weekly basis.
  - expect them to provide evidence of their sales actions and results on a weekly basis.

- expect them to report on their efforts and results at a weekly sales team meeting.
- Explain how you, as team leader, will be reporting on team results to your manager on a monthly basis.
- Explain that the team meeting is an opportunity for all of us to discuss our performance and to suggest ways to improve sales actions and sales results.

ASSESS
- Working together, continually assess how well the team member is performing their sales and service actions.
- Agree any additional training, coaching or other support they require.
- Re-negotiate their action goals as the team member becomes more confident and competent.

PROVIDE RECOGNITION AND FEEDBACK
- Provide weekly and monthly acknowledgement of efforts and results of individuals.

ALL THOSE PEOPLE WHO ARE EXPECTING A BONUS..... STEP FORWARD..... JONES! WHERE THE HELL DO YOU THINK YOU'RE GOING ?!!!...

Managing sales performance 2

What is the nature of the sales and service culture within the area you manage? Have you created an environment which is conducive to optimising sales and service or one which limits the achievement of sales and service outcomes?

This checklist will help you answer those questions and point the way to improved sales and service performance.

OUTCOMES
- Are your overall sales and service outcomes clear to staff?
- Do all staff understand and accept their role in contributing to these outcomes?
- Are the desired outcomes perceived by staff to be realistic?
- Are your sales and service goals periodically reviewed to ensure that they are consistent with customer expectations?

RESOURCES
- Do people have enough time to achieve sales and service goals?
- Are there enough people to provide the level of required sales actions and desired service levels?
- Are there sufficient tools, job aids, equipment, and other resources to achieve the desired level of service?
- Are your resources being spent in areas important to your customers?

BEHAVIOUR
- Can the behaviours that lead to sales and service outcomes be performed?
- Does something in the systems and procedures prevent the behaviour from occurring?
- Are the desired behaviours observable/measurable?
- Are you aware of how your staff perceive the desired sales and service behaviours?
- Are you asking people to compromise their own values?

- Will the behaviours you are targeting result in outcomes that your customers will perceive as value added sales and service?

RESULTS
- Are both quantitative and qualitative results measured?
- Are both outcome and process results measured?
- Are results linked back to appropriate individuals and appropriate behaviour?
- Are customer satisfaction and customer-focused results measured and reported on with the same sense of urgency as financial and productivity results?

FEEDBACK - information
- Is the feedback related to a goal?
- Is the feedback immediate?
- Does the feedback go direct to the appropriate person?
- Does the feedback go to all levels of the organisation?
- Is the feedback graphically displayed?
- Does the feedback indicate how the result is important to the customer?

FEEDBACK - motivation and development
- Are both results and behaviour being reinforced?
- Are both improvement and achievement being reinforced?
- Is the reinforcement specific?
- Is it timely?
- Is it tied to a sales and service goal?
- Is there a proper mix of tangible and intangible, monetary and non-monetary rewards?
- Are rewards based on outcomes that are important to customers?
- Is non performance quickly and supportively confronted?
- Is the performance issue described specifically?
- Are open-ended, future oriented questions used?
- Does feedback and follow-up take place after the discussion?

Hit and miss

If you manage a sales team, here are a number of things to do to improve the achievement of sales targets.

- Agree the monthly and weekly sales targets required to meet the yearly sales target.
- Agree the minimum number of contacts needed each week to meet weekly sales targets.
- Discuss with your sales team ways to improve sales.

DON'T BE DISCOURAGED BY A NEGATIVE RESPONSE ..

- Share success stories within the sales team.
- Agree a sales strategy for use with buyers.
- Agree a list of actions to implement the strategy. Discuss things to say and do.
- Identify which segments of our market buy most product.
- Target those buyers with the highest potential to buy.
- Seek referrals to other buyers from existing buyers.
- Discuss ways to overcome typical objections to buying our product within the sales team.
- Pass on feedback about our products or services to key people.
- Identify customers who use one of our products or services already but who have the potential to use other products or services we provide.
- Discuss ways to identify and contact potential customers within the sales team.
- Develop standard script guidelines with questions to ask which will unearth

known and unknown needs and with benefit statements.
- Obtain lists of potential customers from business and professional associations, the Yellow Pages et al, business directories in libraries, chambers of commerce, etc.
- Develop a contact plan for prospects in the same area to minimise travel time.
- Practise your sales presentation with other team members - learn from each other.
- Discuss the best ways to make the key selling points to obtain sales.
- Review the achievement of sales targets on a weekly basis.
- Agree new actions to put into practice where sales targets are not being achieved.
- Hold monthly in-house coaching sessions using the best ideas from the team to learn techniques which have worked successfully.

There are no hopeless situations; there are only men
who have grown hopeless about them.
Clare Booth Luce
Congresswoman, playwright, and diplomat, Europe in the Spring.

The will to persevere is often the difference between
failure and success.
Davis Sarnoff, 1891-1971
Founder and President, RCA, Wisdom of Sarnoff and the World of RCA.

Most sales(people) try to take the horse to water and make him drink.
Your job is to make the horse thirsty.
Gabriel M. Siegal
President, Medicab of New York, Inc.

Always ask for the business

Most people, the seller the buyer, don't like the 'hard sell' approach adopted by some organisations. And in reality, it is not necessary. You can be very effective at selling by using a 'needs' based approach. If we can get the customer to agree that they have a genuine need, and we can demonstrate to the customer that our product or service meets their need, and we can create a positive emotional response from them, then we'll be a long way down the path to making a sale.

If you manage a sales team, you can use this process to increase sales:
- Convene a meeting with your sales team.
- Discuss the purpose and the agenda for this meeting.
- Provide a list of the selling tips for each person. (see 'Sales Tips')
- Ask all staff to read the tips to add any new ideas and make a note of the ones they think are most effective.
- Add any new ideas to the list.
- Ask each person to nominate 3 to 5 things on which they will concentrate over the next week (including yourself).
- Record these actions against each person's name. Individuals record their actions on an action plan.
- Ask the team to be prepared to come along next week to discuss how, when, how often and with whom they performed these actions. Explain that you'll be doing the same.
- Discuss within the team how to perform these actions. Use coaching and role play.

At the next meeting:
1. Discuss how each of you performed your nominated actions and the results you achieved.
2. Encourage discussion of tactics to allow team members to learn from each other.
    - Select new actions to focus on over the next week or keep the focus on the same actions for the next week, month or whatever.
    - Repeat this process with the team for as long as there is benefit.

SALES TIPS

- Ask open questions to clarify the customer's needs. Listen, paraphrase their needs and ask if they agree that this is what they are looking for.
- Show with your eyes, tone of voice, smile, posture that the customer is welcome.
- Personalise the product - relate your own experience of the product.
- Use language that the customers will understand - avoid jargon.
- Give undivided attention when the customer is talking to you - respond sincerely, don't feign interest or fake it.
- Look for short and long term gains for the customer - establish long term relationships.
- Ask questions to uncover 'unknown' or 'unexpressed' needs.
- Be able to explain the benefits and advantages of our products or services over our competitors.
- Demonstrate a "yes we can" attitude.
- Be reliable - do what you say you will do and check to see that the customer is satisfied.
- Make notes - don't rely on your memory.
- Don't take objections personally - it is not you who they are rejecting (unless you have created a negative emotional response).
- View objections as opportunities.
- Listen carefully for clues as to their 'unexpressed' or 'unknown' needs - look for opportunities.

Gee... I hadn't thought of that

Customers don't always know what it is that they don't know about how our product can help them. That is, they may have needs that they haven't identified yet - 'unknown' needs. Part of the sales person's job is to help a customer identify their needs related to their current and future circumstances. This is not 'hard sell'. We are talking about what they need not what they want.

WHAT CAN I SAY AS THEY WALK OUT THE DOOR?...

One way to do this is by asking the customer 'scenario' questions which cause them to think about a situation they may not have thought about. e.g. "How would you pay your mortgage if you were to lose your job?"

MORE SALES TIPS
- Treat the customer as an individual - how you would like to be treated.
- Remember that they may be your 50th customer for the day, but you may be their first salesperson for the day.
- Offer suggestions and better alternatives.
- Empathise with the customer's objections. Don't argue - agree with them. "Yes. Look if I was in your shoes, I'd probably see it the same way. Let me explain..."
- See 'selling' as something everybody does - it's a way of helping a customer in

need. If you don't help them identify a genuine need now, it may cost them later.

- Don't force the sale - no need, no sale.
- Avoid jargon and 'organisation speak'. It doesn't sound like jargon to us because we use it all the time, but to the customer it can be very confusing. A confused customer is not a buying customer.
- Introduce yourself by name.
- Ask, yourself "what can I say that will make them feel good as they walk out the door?"
- Keep your promises - don't promise what can't be delivered. Don't raise expectations which can't be met.
- Use the customer's name if you know it. If appropriate ask, "May I call you Mrs Martin, or Harry, or whatever?" (Don't call Mrs Martin, Harry.)
- Reinforce facts about the features, advantages and benefits of our products and services.
- Objections are based on the customer's perception, but not all their perceptions are based on facts and often they do not know all the facts about the product and service.
- Allocate time to do 'after sales' follow up activities.
- If you can see a customer is very attracted to a product, confirm it in their mind by saying to them, "You like it don't you?"
- If the sale is stalling, ask "What would you like us to do?"
- Keep product information handy.
- Tell them to contact you personally when they want to go ahead or if they have a query.
- At the conclusion of a sale, thank the customer for their business.
- Ask questions which lead to them agreeing their needs - don't just make statements about the product or service.
- Always show how our features and benefits match their needs.
- Remember that we are the product experts. We will probably know more about what the product can do for them than they will.
- Experiment with different ways of asking questions and with different ways of asking for the business. **And always ask for the business.**

Slimy might sell, but it doesn't stick

Everybody has a story about a slimy salesman. While there are many exceptions, they all too often bob up in the used-car business, real estate, and insurance. But they are not confined to those occupations - they pop up everywhere. We've crossed paths with a couple in our field.

'Slimys' aren't hard to spot. They are lousy listeners, great liars, dripping in insincerity, prone to exaggeration, will say anything that they think you want to hear, will readily compromise their principles (if they have any) for money and have no self awareness - how they come across to others.

The decision to buy is based on emotion as much as it is on logic. How the salesperson is perceived by the customer can have a huge influence on their decision to buy. Keep the customer 'on side' - don't get them 'off side'. Drop the slick sales patter, the insincere compliments, the feigned interest. Be polite, courteous, sincere, genuine, knowledgeable, respectful, attendant, honest and helpful. You'll win more sales and get more intrinsic satisfaction.

AND MORE SALES TIPS
• Ask them, "Will this...(feature or benefit) give you what you need?"

- Have all brochures, product information and applications on hand.
- Fill out the paperwork for them.
- Concentrate on three best selling features and three best selling benefits for each product.
- Maintain the relationship with regular customers by checking on how things are going and is there anything they need. Or better still, ask them a 'scenario' question, "Winter's nearly on us. How much tread is left on your tyres?"
- Offer prospective customers a free second opinion (quote).
- Ask yourself every time, "How can I exceed the customer's expectations?"
- Treat each customer as if they are the only thing happening in your life at that moment.
- Try to establish rapport with the customer rather than just fill in the paperwork.
- Ask questions and establish their needs rather than describe products they may not need.
- Treat each customer as if they were your best friend.
- Speak positively about the organisation you work for and its products and services.
- Avoid talking to other staff members in front of customers.
- If there is a queue of customers, acknowledge them and let them know you won't be long.
- Create advocates of our customers by doing them favours or going out of your way to help them.
- Remember that the customer is not here for us, we are here for them.
- Don't be discouraged by a negative response - ask new questions or rephrase your questions.
- Experiment with different ways of selling your products or services - use what works for you.
- Show you are actively listening by paraphrasing or summarising the customer's needs or requirements - verbally confirm your understanding. Check that you have got it right. Don't make assumptions.
- Know the features, benefits, advantages and conditions of our products.
- **Always, always, ask for the business.**

If you don't know where you're going, it doesn't matter how you get there

Very few businesses operate successfully without a formalised and clear operating strategy. Managers in organisations small and large can apply the following process in identifying their strategic goals.

OBJECTIVES

What is it you want your business to achieve? List the major objectives of your business. These are long term or on-going commitments to bring about a desired state of affairs. Larger organisations will relate to these as their mission statement. An objective is often not associated with a specific time deadline. Objectives may relate to ongoing functions or strategic issues.

SCENARIOS

Consider future scenarios. Forecast the circumstances and document the assumptions under which the business expects to operate. Specifically, scenarios indicate the expected availability of resources. List likely scenarios under two headings - optimistic and pessimistic. For each scenario listed, consider the probability of that scenario actually occurring. Think hypothetically and 'out of left field'.

PRIORITIES

Establish a priority for each objective. Priorities indicate the relative importance of the various objectives in the light of the most likely scenario. Allocate a percentage out of 100 to the most important through to the least important. The total of all priority weightings should equal 100.

STRATEGIES

These are a series of decisions and/or actions designed to create favourable conditions or eliminate potential obstacles to enable the achievement of an objective. A strategy usually involves a major commitment of resources and has a significant potential impact on the success of the organisation.

For each objective, list the major decisions and actions which will need to be undertaken.

PERFORMANCE INDICATORS

For each objective, list the specific things you would expect to see happening if the objective was being achieved.

GOALS

A commitment to bring about a specific, measurable state of affairs in a definite time period. Goals are milestones in the pursuit of objectives. They specify how much of a performance indicator is to be achieved in a particular time period.

For each objective and the associated performance indicators, list goals for the next 12 months or longer term.

EARLY WARNING INDICATORS

Predicting the future is risky business. For each of your worst case scenarios, list the things which could start to happen to indicate that things are changing or deviating from the expected.

Set up a mechanism to monitor these early warning indicators.

Dead man walking

Stress is now known as the silent killer. Many traditional medical practitioners now readily accept that stress (or more importantly, how a person reacts to stress) is a major contributor to illness and disease. Stress is a fact of life. You can't avoid it, you can only react to it in some way or another. Stress is any change that you must adjust to. Both positive events and negative events can produce stress.

Stress takes its toll on all of us, but many of us are unaware of the damage being done to our health. Unfortunately, awareness in the message of a heart attack may be a little too late. However, your body is advising you constantly on how you are handling stress. You don't need to wait for the giant 'tap on the shoulder' of a heart attack - your body is sending you messages all the time.

The trouble is too many managers are unaware of what our bodies are telling us or, worse, ignore the message. These are some of the symptoms of stress:

• tightness in the stomach or chest   • grinding teeth
• shallow breathing   • clamped jaw
• tense muscles   • frequent deep sighing
• slight headaches   • cold, sweaty hands
• rapid breathing   • shaking limbs

In the workplace, managers have an additional stress factor. They are accountable for resolving the 'people' issues within their workforce. Managers who are not dealing with stress effectively make poor managers. Their communicating style, clarity of perception, ability to make decisions and to resolve problems will be seriously impaired.

Ever had this experience? You're running late for work and an important meeting. As you are driving to work you seem to get every red light. If you have to cross a railway line, the boom gates will be down. The car in front of you will have a learner driver or be moving excruciatingly slowly. The cars on the freeway will be moving slower than usual. The traffic jams will be longer and more frequent.

Every donkey behind a wheel will be out driving in front of you. Get the picture? And you're late. And as you sit there and wait for the light to change to green, you're starting to stew. You are getting angry at the traffic lights, at the driver in front of you. You are letting the situation cause you stress. In fact, you caused the situation in the first place by choosing to be late.

Contrast this experience with the time when you are not in a hurry. Everything seems to flow better and you're not getting angry. In all probability, the situations are the same. The only difference will be the images you are creating in your mind in relation to each situation. More on that later. (See 'Mind over matter').

Learn to listen to your body. Your body tells you when you are stressed.

* Focus on your body at least once a day.
* Close your eyes and starting with your toes slowly move up your body. Imagine that part of your body in your mind.
* Slowly sweep up and down your body searching for areas of tension.
* When you locate a tense spot, focus on it so that you become very aware of it.
* Be aware of the muscles in your body that are tense.
* Take a deep breath and as you exhale imagine that the tension is leaving that part of your body.
* Check out how you feel now. Note that you will feel immediately more relaxed. (As always, if pain persists consult your professional health practitioner).

HUDSON... I'M STRESSED!

Mind over matter

> Men are disturbed not by things,
> but by the views which they take of them.
> **Epictetus**
> *c. 60-120 Roman stoic philosopher, Encheiridon.*

> It is not work that kills men; it is worry. Work is healthy; you can hardly
> put more upon a man than he can bear. Worry is rust upon the blade. It
> is not the revolution that destroys the machinery, but the friction.
> **Henry Ward Beecher, 1813-1887**
> *American clergyman, Proverbs from Plymouth Pulpit.*

> Anger is an acid that can do more harm to the vessel in which it's
> stored than to anything on which it's poured.
> **Anonymous**
> *How to Live With Life (Readers Digest, 1965)*

> Anyone can hold the helm when the sea is calm.
> **Pubilius Syrus**
> *c. 42 B.C. Roman Writer, Maxims*

Your mind - the set of thoughts you have about yourself or others in any given situation - is a major player in how stressed you are at work or anywhere. Why is it that some managers show obvious signs of stress in response to a particular situation and other managers remain calm and unstressed in response to the same situation? While there are different schools of thought in answer to that question, I believe that the nature of the thoughts the managers hold about themselves in relation to that situation dictates their level of stress.

Simply put, what you think creates how you feel - think bad, feel bad; think good, feel good. Unfortunately, it's not that simple. It is hard to understand why many people have a propensity to always think the worst in any situation. It is hard to change those people who suffer from chronic depression or violent anger. Yet for most of us it can be a great stress release to see what our mind is doing when we are experiencing stress. We're talking here about stress which is damaging to us or others not the normal stress we need to help us function effectively.

The next time your body tells you that you are experiencing a level of anxiety, anger, frustration or fear etc., and you want to feel less stressed about the situation, try this process:

- Think about the things that are currently happening in your life or imminent things about to happen. They could be work related or unrelated to work.
- Isolate the one situation which is causing you most stress.
- Note where and how you are feeling this stress. Is it a sinking feeling in the stomach, shallowness of breath, a tightness in the chest, a feeling of a weight on your shoulders, etc.?
- Now make a list of the full range of thoughts you have about you and others in the situation. Describe the images in your mind. Write them down randomly - as they come to you, even thoughts that may appear irrelevant. Don't judge them in any way.
- Note how your level of stress changes as you write them down and 'get them off your chest' - or more accurately, get them out of your mind.
- Now go over your list of thoughts and for each thought allocate either the letter (A) or (B). (A) is for thoughts or images that are rational, positive, useful, freeing or functional. (B) is for thoughts or images that are irrational, negative, useless, limiting or dysfunctional.
- Now write these thoughts on to two separate lists - A and B.
- Take the B list and reflect on each thought. Is the thought based on fact or assumption or inference? What is the evidence to support this thought? Is it really true? Where has this thought or image come from? Is the thought based on something that has actually happened or that you imagine could happen?
- Eliminate those thoughts from your B list which crumble into nothingness under this scrutiny or rewrite them to more accurately reflect the facts.
- Focus on your A list. Read and re-read.
- Note how calmer and more clear headed you now are about the situation.

Relaxevous

Here are some simple things that you can do to help alleviate the symptoms of stress at work or at home. These exercises will not remove the cause of the stress, but they will make you feel better, be better able to successfully handle stress and help prevent stress related illness and disease

MEDITATION

The benefits of meditation are now well documented and accepted. Meditation doesn't mean that you have to shave your head, change your belief system and start wearing saffron coloured robes. Meditation can lead to greater enlightenment, but if you have a problem with that for 'meditation' read 'relaxation'. Many successful business people, top sports people and olympic athletes use meditation to enhance their performance.

Just as you create your stress response you can also create your relaxation response. (Adapted from the best selling and highly recommended book by Herbert Benson, MD, 'The Relaxation Response'). The four conditions necessary to bring on your relaxation response are as follows:

1. A quiet environment
   - quiet, calm, no distractions.
2. A mental device
   - A sound, word or phrase repeated silently or aloud, e.g., 'I am calm'. Or fixed gazing at an object, e.g. a candle or a pin-prick hole in the side of a cardboard

box placed over a bright light.
- Repetition of the words or phrases helps prevent distracting thoughts.
- Eyes closed (except if doing open eye meditation).
- Breathe normally but not shallowly.
3. A passive attitude
- Suspend any judgement about what you are doing.
- Most important element.
- Distracting thoughts will occur. Let them - become aware of them and then return to repetition or gazing. This is the hardest part of meditating, but rest assured this affects everybody. With practise you will become better at calming your mind.
- Do not worry about how well you are doing or about those distracting thoughts that keep popping up.
4. A comfortable position
- Any way which is comfortable and relaxed, but you don't want to fall asleep.

DEEP BREATHING

- Try this - it will produce instant relief from stress symptoms such as rage, anger, frustration, anxiety, fear. You can do this sitting at your desk or in your car or while standing up.

- Take a deep, full breath filling the stomach first then the upper lungs. Exhale fully and completely. Keep your mouth closed and inhale and exhale through your nose. If this is uncomfortable for you, open your mouth. Inhale again and mentally count slowly from 1 to 4 while inhaling. Hold your breath and again count slowly from 1 to 4. Slowly count from 1 to 8 while exhaling fully and completely. A couple of practices will show you how slow to count.

- You may have run out of breath before you made it to 8. If you did, try again inhaling deeper and exhaling slower. This exercise is best done with your eyes shut. Repeat the process four times and feel the difference.

Know thyself

Teamwork within the organisation environment can always do with improvement. It is mystifying how unaware some people are of the effect they have on others and the team in general.

In most cases people really believe they are good team members. Most team leaders think likewise. One of the most important tasks team members can perform is to assess what they say and do to assist the team to function.

Here is a list of actions all team members, including the manager, can use to measure the effectiveness of their contribution to the team.

- If you find yourself defending your actions with another person who claims your actions have created extra work for others, swap places. See it from the other's perspective. Check - are you defending yourself legitimately or is your frustration caused by the realisation that they're right? In fact, your own actions really have created a problem.

- Have the courage and integrity to back down and admit it when you are wrong.

- Offer constructive comments to the team rather than destructive comments.

- Allow other team members to present a point of view. Share your ideas with the team.

KEEP A SENSE OF HUMOUR WHEN THINGS BECOME TENSE..

- Contribute to the team without having to be asked.
- Look for things to do to assist others when your workload is quiet.
- Offer to do tasks even though you don't enjoy doing them.
- Encourage others to identify things to improve teamwork.
- Ensure your work is completed to enable the team to function.
- Provide assistance when other team members are under pressure.
- Tolerate other colleagues' deficiencies.
- Provide support to colleagues to enable them to overcome their deficiencies.
- Keep a sense of humour when things become tense.
- Thank colleagues who have helped you in a time of need.
- Think through the consequences of your actions or comments on workmates before acting or speaking.
- Empathise with colleagues who may be having difficulty.
- Identify the hidden issues that may be causing people to behave the way they do.
- Implement ways to improve teamwork.
- Clarify your role and the role of others within the team.
- Act to assist others to implement common goals.
- Accept decisions that you may not have agreed with.
- Offer encouragement to team members.
- Provide constructive feedback on team results.

The point of no return

There are several aspects to technology that make the manager's life a more difficult one.

- It moves quickly - take a few days off and you're being left behind.
- It is beyond the realms of our ability to comprehend how this whole concept works - what knowledge people must possess.
- To maintain understanding of new technological changes requires constant upskilling.
- When a problem arises one can be helpless because of our great dependence on it - it is our major source of information and means of communication.
- To keep abreast is extremely expensive - where are the promised cost savings?
- It can present a moral dilemma - replace staff with automation?
- You are never going to be completely up to date. It's time to upgrade.

So how do we manage this modern day monster? Use it purely as a tool by which you go about your daily work.

Think of it as:
- a friend not an enemy
- useful not useless
- helpful not a hindrance
- constructive not destructive
- a means to an end not the end itself
- the slave not the master
- controllable not controlling

Just how you can do these things may depend on how well the following are performed.

- Identify and discuss the benefits of technology to your work area.
- Clarify and discuss with staff your and their roles in relation to technology and work.
- Identify the latest technology, in consultation with industry experts, in relation

to the key functions of your area.

- Identify and discuss the technological development and training needs of staff.
- Include technological training in the training and development plan.
- Discuss with staff the equipment (hardware and software) needed for the area.
- Discuss with senior management what they need to do to support any training and development initiatives you believe are important.

- Use outside sources to train staff in the use of technology.
- Engage outside sources to talk to your area about the latest relevant technological initiatives.
- Network with other managers from like industries to find out what they are doing in the technology field and how they are doing it.
- Discuss with colleagues the importance of technology and how it can assist you in your professional field.
- Join professional associations and attend professional conferences, particularly when there is a focus on technology in your industry.
- Circulate relevant literature about the related technology.
- Discuss with customers the benefits to them of using the latest technology.
- Encourage staff to mentor and coach other staff members.
- Appoint a technology coordinator or in bigger organisations a technology area.
- Budget for the purchase of the required equipment (hardware and software) needed for your area.

You can't manage time

> Time goes, you say? Ah no!
> Alas, time stays, we go.
> **Austin Dobson**
> *English poet and essayist, The Paradox of Time.*
>
> (Napoleon) directed Bourrienne to leave all his letters
> unopened for three weeks, and then observed with satisfaction how
> large a part of the correspondence had thus been disposed of itself,
> and no longer required an answer.
> **Ralph Waldo Emersom, 1803-1882**
> *American essayist and poet, The Man of the World.*
>
> Selectivity - the determination to choose what we will attempt
> to get done and what we won't - is the only way out of the panic that
> excessive demands on our time can create.
> **Andrew S Grove**
> *CEO, Intel Corp., One-On-One With Andy Grove (G. P. Putnam's Sons, 1987)*

The term 'time management' is a little misleading. Time is a constant - there are 24 hours in the day every day - and you can't manage a constant dimension like time. You can only use it or abuse it. Time management is really about managing yourself and others so that the time available to you is used productively.

During the course of your day, there are many demands and priorities which a manager has to juggle. One measure of how well you use your time is the amount of time you spend on your highest priority activities. Many managers will be shocked to find out how much time they spend on low priority or non-value adding activities.

To find out where your time goes and to help improve your use of time, complete this 'Demand Analysis' on yourself. Do it honestly or you'll waste your time.

- Reproduce the form on the next page. It helps if you can keep your analysis to one to two pages so an A3 size page may work best.
- Using 'brainstorming', make a list of all the demands on your time - daily, weekly, monthly, whatever. Go for quantity, include everything. The more you can list, the more valuable this will be. Be specific about the demand. The demand could be a person or an activity or an event. This is the most important part of your demand analysis, so do it exhaustively. Don't try and do it in sequence. Just list things as they come to you in any order. A useful list will probably contain 30-50 demands.
- Choose an appropriate time period for your calculation - say a week or a month.
- Scan your full list and identify the demand that takes the least amount of your time and allocate a base unit of one (1) point. Now compare each other demand to this one and estimate the amount of time you spend relative to the item which is your base unit.
- For example, if you reckon that you spend twice as much time on a demand compared to your base unit then allocate two points to that item. If you reckon that you spend 20 times as much time on a demand as you spend on your base unit, allocate 20 points to that item. And so on until each demand has been allocated points compared to your base unit of one.
- Add the total number of points. Say it adds up to 280.
- Calculate the percentage of your time you spend on each demand. For example - take the demand on which you spend the least time, i.e. one unit or 1 point. $1 \div 280 \times 100 = 0.4\%$.
- Take the item allocated 20 points. $20 \div 280 \times 100 = 7\%$. Repeat this for all items and record in the 'percentage time' column.
- Next, identify whether the demand is from an internal customer or an external customer. Allocate 'I' or 'E' in this column.
- Cover the 'percentage time' column and allocate a priority to each item as follows: A - most important B - less important C - least important.

Time demand analysis

Ask your work group to conduct their own 'demand analysis' and then discuss the results with a view to managing our time demands more effectively.

Work Priorities

DEMANDS	PRIORITY	CUSTOMER INT/EXT	% TIME
A - most important	B - less important		C - least important

What is your 'demand analysis' telling you about how productively your time is used?

Answer these questions :

- What percentage of your time goes on non-value adding activities?
- What percentage of your time goes on low priority activities?
- What things are low priority for you but high priority for others?
- What things are high priority for you but low priority for others?
- What percentage of your time do you spend on high priority activities related to internal customers?
- What percentage of your time do you spend on high priority activities related to external customers?
- What demands could you stop responding to with little or no consequence?
- What demand priorities do you need to negotiate again with your manager?
- What demand priorities do you need to negotiate again with your staff?
- Which people make the most demands on your time and what are the priorities of those demands?
- What demands on your time could be delegated to your staff?
- Are you able to stay focused on your high priority demands?
- Which demands are routine and expected?
- Which demands are non-routine and unpredictable?
- What do you now need to do to be better focused and to manage your time demands better?

Time saving tips

> There's never enough time to do it right,
> but there's always time to do it over.
> **Jack Bergman**
> *Vice President, Jordache Enterprises Inc. Speech.*
> *Brooklyn, New York, 1987*

Here is a collection of time-saving tips that managers can apply at work.

- Get ideas out of your head - reduce the clutter in your mind. Do your thinking where you can see it. Use a whiteboard or put it down on paper. List the stakeholders who can influence your proposition and the things working for and the things working against it.
- Set up three piles for documents and material crossing your desk. (1) Urgent and important. (2) Important but not urgent. (3). Unimportant and not urgent. Review pile (3) weekly to throw most of it in the bin.
- Keep your work station uncluttered. Only have on your desk things relevant to whatever you are working on at the time. Keep other material handy but out of sight to avoid being distracted. Mess equals chaos and inefficiency.
- Fight the urge to do things on impulse. Have an 'impulse' file. When an impulse hits you write it in your file for later action. Just writing it down reduces the strength of the impulse.
- Write answers to letters and memos on the original, keep a copy for your records and return the original.

> I'm going to stop putting off things starting tomorrow.
> **Sam Levenson, 1911-1980**
> *Teacher and comedian, You Don't Have to be in Who's Who to Know What's What. (Simon & Schuster, 1979).*

- If you spend most of your day sitting, stand up and walk around for a couple of minutes every hour or do some of your work standing.
- Discuss ways we waste time with your staff and agree actions to use our time more effectively.
- Meet people in their office or place of work so that you can leave their office rather than having to wait for them to leave yours.
- Take an overwhelming task, break it up into small parts or steps, decide an order of priority and tackle that big project bit by bit.
- Every day, tackle one task that you find unpleasant or difficult. Have a set time to do this each day.
- Every 12 months, do a 'clean out' of your files. Be hard on the junk you normally hang on to. If you haven't used something in the past 2 years, throw it out.
- Stay focused on your highest priority at any given time during your day. Work on only one task at a time.
- Create a 'worry' list. Jot down those things which are cluttering your mind with worry. Most of them won't happen anyway. You will spend less time being distracted by unproductive thinking. Review your 'worry' list each week.
- Practice self discipline. Write down the things you do which most waste your time and the time of others, e.g. compulsive talking. Keep the list where you can see it. Set small goals to achieve each day, e.g. I will deliberately resist three urges to speak compulsively to my colleagues. Keep a list of the thoughts that pop into your head and discuss them all at once at a later time.
- Constantly ask yourself the question, "What is the best use of my time right now?" Place this question somewhere you can see it at your work station.
- Take time out to relax physically and mentally. Do two, ten minute relaxation exercises every day.

> People who employ their minds too much with trifles
> often make themselves incapable of doing anything serious or great.
> **Francois de La Rochefaucauld, 1613-1680**
> *French politician, writer and philanthropist,*
> *Reflections, or Sentences and Moral Maxims.*

Where does time go?

> Scales and clocks ar-re not to be thrusted to decide
> annything that's worth deciding. Who tells time be a clock? Ivry hour is
> th' same to a clock an' ivry hour is diff'rent to me. Wan long, wan short.
> **Finlay Peter Dunne**
> *'Things Spiritual' Mr Dooley Says (1910)*
>
> The days come and go like muffled and veiled figures sent from a dis-
> tant friendly party, but they say nothing, and if we do not use the gifts
> they bring, they carry them as silently away.
> **Emerson**
> *Journals, 1847*

We cannot manage time ... but we can manage ourselves.

How often do you find that you have too many things to do and not enough time in which to do them? People hounding you - where's this, where's that? Up goes the stress level - sleepless nights follow, our tolerance level drops and everyone suffers.

Balancing organisation life and personal life is a difficult thing to do. Both place demands on us. For those of you who are forever running from point A to point B, take time out to look over these pointers. They just might help you.

- Set aside 15 minutes each day to identify your daily/weekly work requirements.
- Prioritise your work requirements by listing the most important things to do followed by the next most important and so on.
- Do the things which are at the top of your priority list and work your way through the list.
- Minimise unwanted interruptions which reduce productivity by setting aside a

time when you must not be disturbed.

- Prepare staff members for the delegation of duties.
- Delegate work to others who are willing and able.
- Organise your office to ensure ease of location of materials and documents needed to complete your work.
- Remain focused on a particular task until it is completed. Do this by checking that you are doing what you have set out to do and have not been side tracked to a lesser task.
- Provide for breaks, of up to 5 minutes every hour, in your work day to optimise your thinking ability. Get up and walk around the office, stretch, make a call which will be quick but unrelated to what you are doing, get a coffee, see staff who you sent away while you were busy and find out what they wanted.
- Review the effectiveness of your time management. Do this by keeping a time log, analyse what you completed during the day - was it enough? Were you distracted? By what? By whom?
- Ensure you have enough sleep to enable you to cope with your daily work requirements. Calculate how much sleep you require to function effectively and adjust your retirement and rising times accordingly. Catch up on lost sleep over the weekend or during breaks.
- Participate in exercise and recreation/leisure activities as these will help to keep your productivity levels high. Be careful not to let them encroach on your valuable work time.
- Use a diary to plan your time and mark in important events and appointments.
- Use a daily planner to write out your work day in enough detail to allow you to be clear about what you will be doing.
- Use a year planner to gain an overall picture of your work commitments.
- Arrive at work with enough time to prepare for your day. Say 15 minutes before you are scheduled to arrive.
- Say "no" to others when you do not have enough time to help them. Particularly when you are trying to work on a priority area.
- Seek assistance from others when you have too much to do.
- Give yourself 15 minutes of quiet time to reflect on how your day went. Make notes of things to do tomorrow.

Waste not, want not

How much spare time do you have in your day? None? Join the club. Yet why do some managers seem to get more done, to achieve more with the same amount of time, seem less stressed, more in control than others? Who you don't seem to hear saying, "Well, if I had more time I could...".

The fact is that we all have the same amount of time available to us. It is your own thinking and doing which dictates how effectively you use your time. " BULL.....!" I hear you cry in exasperation as you cite your boss, your customers, head office, senior management, your staff, et al. As the reasons why you are flat out with not enough time to get things done.

Fair enough, it's true that people can place constant and unfair demands on your time which leaves you frazzled and exhausted at the end of the day never seeming to catch up with your backlog of work. But until you stand in front of the mirror and recognise that you and you alone ultimately control how you use your time, nothing much will change. Now I admit that this is a hard line to take and I'm sure you can think of situations in which an individual has no control over their time, but read on anyway. And if you think you're wasting your time - take control - stop.

HARNESSING TIME

- Negotiate deadlines with everybody who places a demand on your time. Don't say yes to any time demand that you can't meet without undue stress. If it's your boss, ask what other things can drop back in priority to accommodate this new demand. Or at least cover yourself (take the pressure off) by saying, "No problem. I'll get on to this straight away, but I'll need a few extra days to finish ...... (the current job)."

- At the end of your day, prepare your 'to do' list for tomorrow. List all the things that have to be attended to tomorrow in random order. Then go through each item and allocate priorities A,B or C. Doing it the night before will clear your mind and help you relax overnight. Next day, start with your A's and then your B's. Forget your C's - they weren't important anyway. Place your 'To Do' list somewhere where you can see it all day.

- If your first 'A' task is a complex task - overwhelming in its size - break it down into its constituent parts. All big jobs are made up of a number of little jobs. Describe the little jobs, then decide their order of priority and start with the number one priority 'little job'.

- Analyse that job you've been putting off to find out why. What is that you are fearful of? What is it about the job you don't like? Why? How do you feel when you are actually doing that job? Does it really hurt? Where? How? Is your mind playing games with you and creating an aversion to the job based on what is really a ridiculous or immature notion? Are you aware of how to actualy go about the job? Do you lack the knowledge or skill to do the job? Is it just that there is no excuse at all and you are just avoiding the job because its boring or unpleasant?

- Stay focused on the one job at a time. As you get distracted ask, "what is my priority at this moment?" Jot down distracting but important ideas in your diary to recall later. Repeat an affirmation in your mind to help you stay focussed and to practise self discipline - "That would be fun. That would be interesting, but I want to stay focussed on this right now."

It takes two to tango

How much of your time is wasted through disruption by others? How much time do you spend in conversations with others which achieve nothing of any use? How much time do you spend on low priority activities initiated by someone else?

Social intercourse in the office or workplace is necessary and can be very beneficial, but beware of those people who want to waste your precious time with idle chat. Remember that for these people to waste your time, you have to let them. They can't do it without your permission. The 'drop in' visitor needs you to let them drop in. Every 'interrupter' needs an 'interruptee'.

Here are some things to try to control the 'drop in' visitor:

- Develop a process for screening visitors. Make sure that your 'open door' policy is not being abused. Get visitors used to the habit of making appointments.
- Don't look up when you hear the office 'chatter-box' is heading your way. Keep your head down and look pre-occupied. Frown.
- When it is absolutely important that you are not disturbed, use a colour-coded tag on the door. A red tag means 'not to be disturbed' and a green tag means 'visitors are welcome'. Explain to staff what the tags mean and clarify any events which would be exceptions to the red tag.
- Use your morning and afternoon tea breaks or lunch breaks as your socialising periods. Do it away from your workstation.
- When delegating, ensure that people are clear on what authority they have to make decisions without constant reference to you. Clarify the types of situations which you expect them to deal with and the type they should refer to you.
- When staff bring problems to you which they are capable of resolving, show them a problem solving process (See 'Get the monkeys off your back') but don't accept the problem as your own nor solve it for them.
- With the 'chatter-box', get in first. "Hey Bill. Good to see you. Sorry mate, can't stop. I've got a deadline to meet and I'm way behind. I'll catch you later"

as you unlock eye-contact and swivel away to reach for a file or tool or something.

- Be alert. When an unnecessary visitor drops in start focussing on tactfully terminating the conversation as soon as it turns social.
- Ask your staff to only report to you when things change from what was agreed or planned.
- Apply the 'Pareto Principle' to your visitors. Keep a list of visitors over a typical week and think of ways to reduce the visits by the 20% who make 80% of the interruptions.
- Take control of visits by being the one to end discussion. Have someone else politely interrupt or phone you at a pre-arranged time to remind you of another appointment.
- Stand up as the visitor enters, remain standing during the conversation then start moving toward the door when you wish to end the discussion.
- Take the initiative by going to the other's workplace so that they can't trap you in yours.
- When all else fails, try borrowing $20 from the chronic visitor everytime she or he visits.

241

Patience is a virtue

If you will please people,
you must please them in their own way;
and as you cannot make them what they should be,
you must take them as they are.
Lord Chesterfield
Letters to His Son, Dec. 5, 1749

Sometimes with secret pride I sigh
to think how tolerant am I;
Then wonder which is really mine;
Tolerance or a rubber spine?
Odgden Nash
'Yes and No', I'm a Stranger Here Myself

We shall sooner have the fowl by hatching the egg than by smashing it.
Abraham Lincoln
Speech, April 11, 1865

Some people have an ability to tolerate fools more readily than others. Is this because it matters to them that they are liked by everyone?

Those people who do not suffer fools lightly, more often than not, couldn't care less what people think about them. Or they may take a view that to get the job done they do not need to put up with the 'rubbish' that is often spoken by these offending individuals. Whilst this attitude may have an upside it also has a downside. Consider the consequences if managers are openly aggressive, rude, intolerant, abrasive or impatient with either customers, colleagues or staff. Like it or not, sometimes we have to bite our tongue and humour the individual in question; for the good of all.

Just how do people, who seem to be unruffled by the irritating few, do it? What mental thoughts do they possess that help them get through the conversation?

If you are prone to low tolerance try some of these thoughts and actions.
- I am only going to be with this person for 'x' minutes.
- I know they are different to me, but let's look at the positive things they are saying.
- I am going to control the conversation by sticking to the point in question, setting the agenda, establishing and agreeing the time we will have together and bringing them back on task should they deviate.
- I will filter only the information I need. The rest will flow straight through. What they are saying is not personal and therefore does not need to ignite any negative thinking.
- I know this person is like this. I have an expectation, therefore, that I can handle it. To get angry or irritated will be a weakness on my part and I am better than that.
- When they do things which annoy me I will say ...... or do ...... to counter its negative effect.

Or try thinking about these.
- Is it worth giving this person a hard time if the long term consequences are going to be worse?
- Identify the specific things which annoy you and ask them if you can have a frank discussion about how it affects you. Once this has happened discuss what alternative things they could do in place of that offending behaviour.
- You may use humour to dismiss the 'ridiculous' things they say. You may change the subject to allow you to 'catch your breath' by saying "look, George, I'm just going to get a coffee would you like one?"
- Identify the underlying motive for their manner. Analyse this and draw a firm conclusion as to why they are like they are. When they do something which 'bugs' you, you have then got a rational reason for their 'irrational' behaviour.
- Ask other people how they refrain from 'losing it' with this person. Ask them what thoughts go through their minds when they are talking to them.
- Consider what the consequences are for you of the relationship not working. If the consequences are serious keep reminding yourself of this and adjust your behaviour accordingly.

We must keep topping up the well

> Education makes people easy to lead,
> but difficult to drive; easy to govern, but impossible to enslave.
> **Lord Brougham**
> *Speech, House of Commons, Jan 29, 1828*
>
> Never believe on faith,
> see for yourself!
> What you yourself don't learn
> you don't know.
> **Bertholt Brecht**
> *The Mother (1932), 6, tr. Lee Baxandall*

Constant involvement of staff in training and development activities provides them with the opportunity to:

- **learn new strategies**
- **explore changes**
- **review different ways to enhance their effectiveness**
- **broaden their thinking**

The world is changing around them and there is an expectation that they are able to meet the needs of the modern business world.

As a manager, it is our professional duty to ensure that we are updating the skills and knowledge of staff at every opportunity.

- Identify the specific training and development needs of staff.
- Discuss with staff your thoughts about their training and development needs.

- Prepare a yearly staff professional and personal development plan.
- Promote and inform staff of forthcoming training and development programs.
- Follow your prepared training and development plan.
- Budget for future training and development needs.
- Encourage staff to involve themselves as mentors in developing their colleagues.
- Encourage staff to establish an area of specific expertise in which they can become an authority.
- Establish training and development priorities for staff which link into the organisation strategic plan.
- Reward and acknowledge staff who develop their skills.
- Identify the multi-skilling needs of staff.
- Build these multi-skilling needs into the training and development plan.
- Provide coaching and mentoring to staff either through yourself or another staff member.
- Provide quality 'off-the-job' training and development programs.
- Discuss, prior to their involvement, why staff are being trained and what is expected of them.
- After training, ask staff how they will apply their new skills and knowledge back at work.
- Provide ongoing refresher courses relating to key skills.
- Monitor how well the training is being applied back at work.
- Report back to staff and colleagues your experiences and learnings from any training and development activities you have recently undertaken.

Awareness precedes all learning

> Training frequently fails to pay off in behavioural changes on the job; Trainees go back to work and do it the way they've always done it instead of the way you taught them to do it.
>
> **Ruth Clark**
> *Manager, Training and Information Services*
> *California Edison Co. Training, November, 1986.*
>
> There is a remarkable agreement upon the definition of learning as being reflected in a change of behaviour as the result of experience.
>
> **E. A. Haggard**
> *Quoted in Readings in Human Learning (McCoy, 1963).*

The biggest problem with non-technical training is the transfer of learning from the training room to the workplace. People are sent off to a training experience for two or three days, return to work and nothing changes. Why is this so?

Is it the fault of the training or the trainers? Possibly - but probably not. The fault lays more in the work environment, not the training environment. Specifically, a major cause of this problem is the actions of line management or, more correctly, the lack of actions of line management.

If 'awareness does precede all learning', then before a person attends a training activity she or he must be convinced of their skill deficiency. That is, they need concrete evidence or examples of things they do which are below standard. Or they need to be clear on exactly what is expected of them once they return from the training.

Every person in your organisation believes that he or she does a good job. None of your employees believe that they are inefficient, unproductive, incompetent or below standard. Yet every single person can nominate some other person whose performance needs to be improved.

A person's perception is their reality. If you don't change their mindset and make them aware of the new, different and better behaviours you expect from them as a result of training, you are contributing to a likely waste of time, effort and money.

Here are some of the reasons why people don't apply the training back on the job :

- No awareness of deficiencies. No acceptance that they have a need to learn anything. (This is good stuff, but I do all of this anyway. It's a good thing Harry is here though - he really needs this).
- No expectation created by their manager of what they will be required to do as a result of the training which is new, different and better.
- No clarification of the behaviour change they will be expected to demonstrate.
- No clarification of how their manager will act to support them in the application of new behaviours.
- No follow-up, monitoring or measurement of expected behaviour change by the manager.
- No discussion with the manager about what they learned from the training and how they will apply those learnings.
- No re-allocation of their work priorities to enable them time to implement new ways of doing things.
- No re-allocation of their workload while they are away attending the training so that they don't return to a backlog of work which demands their attention.
- No mentoring provided by their manager to assist with their learnings and to encourage implementation in the workplace.
- No understanding of the reasons why they have been chosen to attend this training,
- No established work context for the training.

You only play as you train

On-the-job training is the cheapest and most effective way to improve the performance of your team or work group. The person conducting the training needs to be competent in the task in which people are being trained and they need to be effective communicators. The manager may be the on-the-job trainer or this function could be delegated to a member of the team.

The main trap in conducting any form of training is an over reliance on words - too much talking. The amount of information which people retain from just hearing words is very limited. Yet when people are conducting training they invariably fall into this trap - talk, talk, talk.

People learn best through doing not by being told. The focus should be on the trainee not the trainer. The trainee needs to be an active participant in the training, not a passive listener, if you want them to be able and motivated to apply new skills.

Here are some pointers to improve the quality of on-the-job training:

- People learn best by doing. Every time you tell a trainee how to do something, provide the opportunity for applying it immediately - 'hands on' practice.
- If this is not practical, get them to describe in their own words how to do what you just told them. Or they can tell you why it's important to do something this way or that. Or they can tell you what would happen if it were done this way or that.
- Check out their knowledge and experience of the task. It is better to start at a basic level rather than an advanced level. Explain to the trainee at what level you are conducting the training and check frequently if your level of presentation is too basic or too advanced.
- Before starting the training, describe what the learning objective is. State what they will be able to do as a result of the training in observable and measurable terms. Describe how well, that is, to what standard, they will be required to perform the task.

- Job behaviour consists of three parts - knowledge, attitude and skill. To be effective, training must address all three...what the trainee knows, how the trainee feels and what skills the trainee has. Most on-the-job training ignores the critical attitude component. To put it even more simply, job performance requires skill and will. Most performance problems are due to a lack of will not a lack of skill.
- Training should consist of: **S stimulus** (anything you tell or show the trainee); **R response** (what the trainee says or does); and **F feedback** (any corrective comments or actions you make).
- This **S R F** unit is the basic building block of any on-the-job training. An effective training sequence consists of a number of S R F links. Training sequence = SRF + SRF + SRF + SRF + SRF + SRF + SRF....
- The S (stimulus) needs to be short so that the R (response) can be immediate. Any S (stimulus) that you give a trainee should be put to use by the trainee as soon as possible. The emphasis needs to be on the trainee talking and doing rather than the trainer talking and doing.
- The things the trainer says or does (S) are interesting, but the responses the trainee makes (R) are more relevant since these determine the effectiveness of the training.

I COULD HAVE TOLD YOU NOT TO GO NEAR THE GRINDER, BUT IT'S BEST TO LEARN BY EXPERIENCE!......CHAPPY'S NOT EVEN LISTENING...... Damned ungrateful...

ACME MEAT GRINDER
Mark II Pat Pend.

Plan before you train

The best place for staff to learn and develop new skills is at work. While off-the-job training is important in the development of new skills and knowledge, it usually lags behind effective on-the-job training. However, there's the catch. Most on-the-job training is of the unplanned, ad hoc variety and therein lies the problem.

Before you start to train :

- Establish what the trainee already knows about the subject.
- Identify those skills already present which you will build on.
- Establish at what level the trainee is ready to start.
- Decide what attitudes the trainee holds to the job, your organisation, work in general and this subject in particular.
- Decide how this will affect the trainee's ability to learn and what you will say to motivate him or her to learn. How will you get the psychological 'buy in'? How will you answer the question, "What's in it for me?"
- Decide if this is the right person, i.e. are they trainable within your time/money constraints.
- Describe what you want the trainee to be able to do as a result of this training.
- Identify the performance criteria (quality standards) the trainee will be expected to meet.
- Write training objectives that are observable and measurable.

- Decide what the consequences are for correct and incorrect performance.
- Establish what information the trainee needs in order to be able to perform as desired.
- Decide what the trainee must know during the first few weeks or months on the job versus things they can learn later after being in the job for a while.
- Prepare any materials you will need to support the training.
- Prepare a basic session plan with small chunks of talking and showing by you and large chunks of doing by the trainee reinforced with feedback and encouragement from you. Remember that people learn best not by being told but by experiencing the consequences of their actions.
- Organise the workplace and others so that you will not be distracted when training.
- Decide if you are the best person to conduct the training in terms of patience, communicating ability, competence and ability to put yourself in the trainee's mind.

Every moment spent in planning
saves three or four spent in execution.
Crawford Greenwalt
President, Du Pont, Mackenzie,
The Time Trap, (McGraw-Hill, 1972).

Training is important,
but we can't stop production

Managers hold some funny attitudes about training. Some managers believe that if there is a problem in the workplace then all you have to do is to send people off to a training course and the problem is fixed. Others will tell you that they fully support training, but when crunch time comes and opportunity presents, they will give you plenty of reasons why they can't release their staff right now. And, of course, there never is a 'right' time.

Another view is that training is a waste of time, effort and money because managers don't see any change in behaviour after staff have been trained. They may well be right too, but I'll bet that they don't see that they are a major reason for this happening.

All problems have a solution with a cost. If managers want to see new, different and better behaviours resulting from training, then it will cost them some of their time. But time well spent.

For training to be applied in the workplace there needs to be a context, a reason, a purpose, an expectation and a follow-up strategy. Who should do this? The trainers - right? Wrong - the manager.

Before you send your staff off to a training course, meet with them, do these things and watch the difference:

- Think about all the aspects of a person's job performance and identify the areas they need to improve.
- Describe specifically what new skills you want the person(s) to acquire or what things you want the person(s) to do new, different and better.
- Inform yourself about the learning outcomes and the content of the training to make sure the training is relevant.
- Create a context for this particular training - why the training is relevant to them.
- Establish a reason why they have been selected to attend the training. What's the purpose for them and for others with whom they interact.
- State clearly your expectations of what you would like them to get from the training and, most importantly, your expectations of the things you will expect them to begin to do new, different and better back in the workplace.
- Ask them to identify the areas of their job performance that they would like to improve as a result of the training.
- Explain that the training is not a 'punishment' but a development opportunity. Ask them about their attitude to the training and explore any negative views they might hold.
- Agree how their workload will be handled while they are away. Ask what support is needed from you.
- Set up a meeting to review the training the day after it finishes

Inspect the expected

When staff return to the workplace after a high quality training course, they will have undergone some change, however small. They will have learned and experienced some new ways of thinking and doing. They will have some new awareness, some new insights, some new skills. Now they need an opportunity and a motive to practise these new learnings, these new behaviours.

But what have the rest of the staff been doing while they have been away? Busy beavering away at maintaining the status quo. So while the 'trainee' has changed and has some ideas about new ways of doing things, the rest of the gang are unchanged and are maintaining the routine and habit - the old ways of doing things.

The 'trainee' probably comes back to a backlog of work and urgent priorities which demand their attention. Under these conditions, we expect them to apply the learnings from the training course. And this is one of the major reasons why staff don't demonstrate new behaviours after a training course. They come back to a work environment unsupportive of change.

As a manager, to overcome this, try these actions:

- Meet with staff the day after they return from a training course. Set this up in advance so they know you will be meeting with them.
- Ask them what things they gained most from the course - new insights, new awareness, new knowledge, new skills, new perceptions, etc.
- Ask them how they would like to apply these learnings. What things they intend to do which will be new, different and better.
- Re-state clearly your expectations about what changes you will be looking for both in their behaviour and in their results.
- Help them to develop a list of actions they plan to apply.
- Check whether you need to re-arrange the priorities of their workload to allow them time to introduce some new ways of doing things.

- Ask them what they would like you to do more of or less of to assist them to apply their learnings.
- Discuss whether there are existing policies, systems and procedures which will block the application of desirable learnings.
- Discuss with other staff what things the 'trainee' will be doing which will be new, different and better and ask them to support the 'trainee' in the application of these new ways.
- Agree an action plan with the trainee and include regular meetings to monitor and review their progress and to address any on-going problems. Discuss any new experiences, new insights or new consequences as time progresses.
- Encourage them to make small step improvements to the way they do things and look for opportunities to provide recognition and feedback.

No pain, no gain

There is a figure bandied around by proponents of Quality Management and Quality Assurance that relates to organisations of approximately 50 employees or more. They claim that 30% of the activities of the workforce are wasted. That is, that they add no value to the finished product or service.

Imagine the impact in your organisation of your workforce spending 30% of their time engaged in non-productive activities - 30% of your salaries expenditure wasted.

What is causing this waste? Simply put - systems error and human error. That is, inefficient systems and procedures and incompetent people. What's the solution? In the latter case, there's only one answer - training, training and more training. But not the type of training that doesn't change behaviour. That's history. You, the manager, may have been part of the reason why training didn't seem to make much difference in the past. If you want training to be effective in your workplace, you need to take a pro-active role. Here are some things to do:

- Consider the current and future competency requirements of the people in your group or team. That is, what are the things that your people need to be able and willing to know and do now and over the next, say, two years. Make a list - it might have 30 - 50 competencies. Be specific, don't put things like 'communication skills'.

- Assess each person against each competency listed. Use a rating scale - 1 (low competence)

256

through to 5 (high competence) or something that works for you.

- Involve team members and ask them to do a self-assessment using the same competencies list.

- Compare your assessment and their assessment and discuss any major differences.

- Identify the high priority training needs for the team collectively and for each individual.

- Identify training opportunities provided by internal and external training providers or discuss your training needs with your training personnel. Find out when decisions are made regarding training and training budgets.

- Prepare a training plan - what, where, when, for whom, by whom.

- Establish training priorities for staff. Discuss the plan with staff.

- Advise your manager of your training and budget requirements.

- Assess whether you can provide training opportunities using the existing skills within the team.

- Arrange mentors or coaches using your best performers to train others.

- Encourage staff to involve themselves in developing their co-workers.

- Recognise and acknowledge staff who seek out ways to develop their skills.

- Raise the profile and seriousness of training in your area by following the actions listed under, 'You only play as you train', 'Awareness precedes all learning' and 'Inspect the expected'.

The mission is missin'

> What makes life dreary is the want of a motive.
> **George Eliot, 1819-1880**
> *English novelist, essayist, and editor Daniel Deronda*
>
> Where there is no vision, the people perish.
> **Old testament, proverbs 29:18**
>
> Ready! Fire! Aim!
> **Anonymous**

How inspiring is your company vision or mission statement? What impact does it have on the motivation, commitment and desire to excel of employees in the workplace?

Too many vision statements are a waste of time and money. Workers ignore them, deride them and are certainly unmoved by them.

In the worst case, senior management have a weekend away at a luxury resort and come up with a statement of meaningless cliches which are about as compelling as boiled tripe. These are then printed and framed and displayed around the organisation for the benefit of staff and customers alike. As soon as they go up, people grow a foot taller and productivity takes off like a rocket. You wish.

How much impact do these commonly used mission statements really have on employees in the workplace?

'To achieve world's best practice.' 'To achieve excellence in customer service.'

Vision and mission statements are meant to galvanise people, to focus energy, to give meaning and purpose, to inspire and motivate, to make people want to contribute.

It is important for senior management to come up with the grand vision for the organisation, but that's only half the battle. The other half is making it meaningful and compelling to workers at all levels in the organisation.

Why not let teams and work groups come up with their own mission statement and guiding principles for their work area. They can start with the grand mission and guiding principles for the whole organisation and make it meaningful and compelling to them at their level.

Set up a meeting with staff or representatives of staff and take them through this process. (Or use an expert facilitator). Remember to keep it simple.

Team Mission
- Agree the purpose of our team - a statement of the principle activity of our team.

Values
- Agree what our team stands for and what we believe in - for example - trust, openness, equality, fairness, co-operation, improvement, etc.

Guiding Principles
- These guide our relationships with our customers and with ourselves.

Document these statements on to one page and review them regularly with your work group.

The straw that broke the camel's back

> Men for the sake of getting a living, forget to live.
> **Margaret Fuller**
> *Summer on the Lakes (1844), 7*
>
> What is work? and what is not work? Are questions that
> perplex the wisest of men.
> **Bhagavadgita**
> *4, tr. P. Lal.*

Work harder - work smarter - lift productivity - reduce costs - increase profits. Wipe that sweat off your brow. There has to be an easier way of achieving the seemingly impossible without 'flogging' your staff to death. How do we reduce the workload / overload that is encroaching on the worklives of the workforce?

What's that? You're not worried? They're there to work and that's what they're paid for. Correct, but you may like to consider how this perception of overload can be alleviated. It was, after all, but one straw that broke the camel's back.

- Discuss with staff their current work activities, i.e. the current things they do that are important to their job and then identify more efficient ways of performing these activities.
- Identify staff who believe they have an overload of work and discuss what things they do that are extra, outside their role, a waste of time, someone else's job or a low priority.
- Remind staff to continually ask the question "Is this the best use of my time?"
- Identify staff who have spare capacity to do extra (they do exist) and then negotiate what extra things they can take from those staff who are overloaded.
- Agree which jobs / tasks could be allocated to another person. They must be

jobs which can be managed as 'stand alone' tasks. Don't always 'palm off' the mundane and boring tasks or else you will destroy their motivation to work.

- Ensure that the other person is capable and willing to perform these allocated tasks.
- Check whether the way staff do things is contributing to a work overload. Perhaps the current procedures are causing double handling or could be refined to allow one person to make decisions and thus alleviate extra steps in the process.
- Re-assess the priorities of their current workload. It is important to continually check the importance of what they are doing. It is easy to give too much attention to tasks that are not really important. Low importance means low priority for completion.
- Use time management tools to plan for the completion of the key regular tasks that have to be performed. Show staff how to use these tools.
- Ensure others are aware of a genuine work overload of particular staff and discuss with them the best way to alleviate the problem.
- Acknowledge and reward staff who seek to assist others to reduce their workload.
- Ask staff how we can all help each other to ensure that a team member is not overloaded. Ensure staff understand and accept the need to ensure the workload is evenly shared by all staff.
- Discuss with senior management the actions you require from them to assist you to reduce staff workload / overload.
- Involve staff in the implementation of actions to reduce workloads. There is no point identifying solutions to a problem if you are not going to implement them.
- Monitor the implementation of actions to check that work overload is reduced. Do this by asking the staff member what improvement has taken place.
- Negotiate changes with other areas whose actions are contributing to work overload. It may mean others have to do things differently to reduce the over load of staff in your area.

The penis mightier than the sword

Now is not that an attention grabber? Mind you, initially, it was unintentional and when I looked at it, it certainly made me look again.

Gaining the attention of the reader is an important part of writing. As a key means of communicating, we write to do the things that the spoken word can't do. Chiefly, to have a record of the communication that has transpired.

We write to:
- request information or action and
- provide information

When writing consider the following:
- Who will read it
- The key points you want to covey
- The main action you require from the reader - should there be any.
- The format or genre that the written message should take, e.g. memo, letter, e-mail, newsletter, survey, report.
- The confidentiality of the information being imparted or required.

When writing to get the final, 'perfect' copy there are some simple steps to take.
- Draft your first copy by writing out a rough transcript of what you want to 'say'.
- If you are writing a large report, break it into sections, i.e. findings,

recommendations, summary, data, etc. and treat each as a separate article.

- Read what you have written and look for obvious spelling mistakes, grammatical errors, 'typos' and poorly worded text.
- Change any obvious errors to their correct form.
- Check for meaning, clarity, intent, succinctness, interest.
- Use a dictionary or a thesaurus if you can't think of the right word or have used a word that doesn't quite capture what you want to say.
- Experiment and brainstorm different ways of writing the same thing until you come up with exactly what you want.
- Ask other people how they might express something.
- Use quotes to capture the heart of the point you are making.
- Use humour to create interest in the writing (easier said than done).
- Include an opening statement that has a 'hook', eg. something that will grab the reader's attention.
- Rewrite text that you have started but are having trouble finishing or finding the right words. If you don't, it narrows your thinking.
- Avoid using jargon, uncommon or unfamiliar words, and undefined acronyms.
- Check that the level of difficulty in your writing is appropriate for the intended reader.
- Write in point format to make the writing succinct and easy to read.

When using a word processor
- Use the 'spell check' and 'grammar check' facilities.
- Print out a draft copy to read before editing.
- Use a font size that is easy to read - 12pt or greater.
- Set the margins so that there is 'ample' white space around the text - 2 cm to 3 cm is usually easy on the eye.
- Space lines so enough white space exists between them.

Write right

> That writer does the most who gives his reader
> the most knowledge, and takes from him the least time.
> **Charles Caleb Colton, c. 1780-1832**
> *English cleric, sportsman, and wine merchant. Lacon.*
>
> In language it is simply required that it conveys the meaning.
> **Confucius, c. 551-c. 479 B.C.**
> *Chinese philosopher and teacher. Analects.*
>
> Therefore, since brevity is the soul of wit,
> And tediousness the limbs and outward flourishes,
> I will be brief.
> **William Shakespeare, 1564-1616**
> *English dramatist and poet, Hamlet.*

When managers speak, their words, though possibly not forgotten, will disappear into the ether leaving no permanent record to praise or condemn them. However, when managers commit their thoughts to print, their competence may be on permanent display. For that reason alone it is important that a manager develops skill in written communication.

Preparation
- Why am I writing? What do I want to achieve by writing?
- What actions do I want to occur as a result of writing?
- What facts do I want to convey?
- What opinions do I want to convey?
- How much does the reader know about the topic?
- How will I get their attention in the first paragraph and create a desire to read on?

- Why is it important that they read the letter or memo?

Getting started
- On a blank sheet of paper describe the topic in two to three words.
- Using the brainstorming technique, write down any thoughts that come to your mind. Write a few key words only that relate to the thought. Write randomly and quickly. Suspend judgement. Just try to write down all your thoughts as fast as you can. Anything goes. Go for quantity.
- Now go through each item on your list and delete those that are not relevant to your topic or to your purpose.
- Now look at the remaining items and put them into a logical sequence. What is the first thing you want to write? Write the number '1' alongside that item. Now what's the obvious thing to write next? Write the number '2' alongside that item, etc.
- Each item becomes the topic of each paragraph.
- Now you have the structure for your letter or memo with a logical sequence of thoughts.

Check
- Does each paragraph lead on to the next?
- Have I clearly stated what needs to happen in the last paragraph?
- Have I clearly stated what I will do?
- Have I clearly stated what I would like the reader to do?
- Have I used sub-headings and highlights?

8 Rules
- Decide what to say.
- Put it in sequence.
- A paragraph for each step.
- Immediately identify the subject.
- End by pointing the way ahead.
- Use short simple sentences.
- Use punctuation to help understanding.
- Use short words.

Afterword - the new way to manage

The role of the manager has changed dramatically from what it was 10 or 20 years ago. Back then, a manager had to be, primarily, technically good at their job. If they had some people skills too, well, that was a bonus. Nowadays, a manager's focus is more on managing the human and conceptual issues which impact on the delivery of high quality products and services. Today's managers still need to be technically competent, but they require a broader and different set of management skills than their counterpart of yesterday.

Fortunately, the basics of managing people haven't changed too much. The adage, 'treat people reasonably and fairly and most of them respond reasonably and fairly' still prevails.

However, because of the changes in society and the marketplace - a better educated workforce, different expectations and attitudes of the workforce, new safety and environmental laws, increased technology, new industrial relations practices, increased competition, increased cost cutting, increased job mobility, greater consumer awareness and expectations, globalization and, hopefully, greater awareness and enlightenment about the management of our workforce - the focus of today's manager is more likely to be on the following :

- How to constantly get more out of less - less money, less staff.
- How to get staff to embrace, adapt to and willingly implement constant requirements for change.
- How to manage consultation.
- How to establish a process to get staff willingly and actively involved in continuous improvement.
- If people behave according to how they perceive everything, how to incorporate their perceptions in the day to day management of the organisation.
- How to remove fear from the workplace.
- How to manage staff so that they act of their own volition to improve profitability and productivity.
- How to manage and improve team performance through the active participation of team members.
- How to create an environment where team members learn from each other.
- How to get ownership and commitment to focus on the critical areas most requiring action.
- How to harness the power of the team to use peer group pressure as a constructive agent for positive change.
- How to change behaviour in the workplace.
- How to carry out a role with a greater emphasis on facilitation and support.
- How to set up and manage 'self-managing' teams.

I have been learning how to answer these questions for nearly twenty years and Steve Godden and I have attempted to describe these and his learnings in this book. However, I was not satisfied to just put these ideas into a book. I wanted to try something else. I wanted to design and develop **a new management tool - a process which both managers and staff would gladly use and which would address each of the above questions. Hence, the M•A•P•P™ System was born.**

I had long been critical of the traditional ways organisations had tried to change behaviour. As a management consultant, I had first hand experience. I and my ways of thinking and doing were often part of the problem. This had been frustrating me for years because I knew that there had to be a better way. So, just like in the cartoons, one day I was sitting at my desk when I had a sudden flash. At last - a breakthrough!

This simple idea (how often are the best ideas the simple ones?) became the embryo for the current M•A•P•P™ System. But not without a long and frustrating gestation. As usual, I had to overcome the knockers - people with whom I worked who couldn't grasp the concept. But this was the least of my worries. From the moment we began marketing the early version of our new management tool, we attracted huge interest within Australia and overseas. With great expectations, we waited for the flood of orders. Alas - no flood, just a trickle.

The downside of this was that we very nearly went broke. The upside was that, thinking there must be something wrong with the M•A•P•P• System, we kept on developing it, refining it and improving it. Eventually, the true reasons for the lack of sales dawned.

One - I was a lousy salesman. Two - our process was new, innovative and different to what the managers with whom we were negotiating were used to. At the time, it was also unproven. So for mangers to agree to buy our product, they had to step outside their 'comfort zone' and take a risk. We then discovered an interesting and revealing situation. Senior managers would rather spend their money on strategies that were demonstrably ineffective and too often a waste of time, effort and money, but with which everybody was familiar and used to, because it was 'safe'. Hmm.

Happy ending. Gradually, persistence and determination paid off and we can now add 'tried, tested and proven' to our statements of facts about the M•A•P•P™ System.

Now the great and inspiring Dr Ken Blanchard, who was lecturing me and other students on the topic of leadership at the time, once said to me (and the others), "If you don't blow your own bugle, somebody will come and use it for a spittoon."

However, far be it from me to blow the bugle on the M•A•P•P™ System. So, if you are interested, here's what managers and staff have to say about it :

"Fantastic. This is simply fantastic."

"Where was this process twenty years ago?"

"After six months of using this process, we are more than ever convinced that this is the way to go."

"The M•A•P•P™ System has become a valued part of our self evaluation and improvement of our performance."

"I found the exchange of perceptions mildly threatening, but in the end I found it to be an extremely satisfying experience."

"We are very pleased with both the process and the results of our Team Improvement Program using the M•A•P•P™ System ..... Congratulations on developing a process that actually delivers."

".... On the basis of our evaluation, we have decided to extend the application of the system to 50 additional staff incorporating six new work teams."

"Having now been using the M•A•P•P™ System for three months, I am happy to describe both the process and the results as brilliant. There has been a significant improvement in both communication and motivation since we started using this process. I recommend the M•A•P•P™ System without reservation."

"This is a process which we will definitely use as a standard way to improve our business. I recommend the M•A•P•P™ System to any organisation. Thank you!"

".... This system has exciting potential in application to a wide range of industry for improving the performance of individuals and teams."

"The general response from the many managers who examined the M•A•P•P™ System is that it provides a simple yet comprehensive approach that effectively facilitates the drive for a quality culture. This is achieved through a well conceived, action-based, continuous improvement process which utilises peer group pressure to monitor and achieve positive results."

About the M•A•P•P™ System

- Created and designed by Dan Kehoe and Steve Godden.

- It incorporates the philosophy and actions of "You lead, they'll follow" into a 'system' which is applied in the workplace and in which all managers and staff participate.

- It is a very powerful management tool - a process which actively involves both managers and team members or work groups in an action-based process.

- It provides a focus and a framework to improve any aspect of organisation performance.

- It is well accepted by both managers and staff alike.

- It is tried, tested and proven to deliver results.

- It works on the premises that :
  - People will only do willingly those things they value
  - People act according to how they perceive things
  - The two major external influences on a person's behaviour are :
    1. their workmates
    2. their manager

- It gives work teams the power and motivation to improve things which are crucial to the profitability and productivity of the organisation.

- It results in all people doing new, different and better things than is currently happening.

- It is an on-going process that becomes a standard practice in your culture.

- It is a self-managing process.

If you would like to know more about the peaceful revolution of the M•A•P•P™ System, please call Dan Kehoe or Steve Godden on freecall 1800 1800 42 (within Australia) or +(618) 9284 0039 outside Australia or e-mail msi@iexpress.net.au

Management In Action Workshops

Training and development workshops based on the philosophy and actions of "You lead, they'll follow".

- A series of workshops ranging from 1 to 5 days duration.

- Each workshop customised to your needs.

- Can be tailored to suit experienced, new or aspiring managers and team leaders.

- Conducted as interactive workshops using real situations from the client organisation.

- All participants receive a free copy of "You lead, they'll follow" for workshops of 2 days or longer.

- Maximum of 20 participants per workshop.

TRANSFER OF LEARNING FROM TRAINING ROOM BACK INTO WORKPLACE

- Pre-workshop assessment of participant's needs.

- 'Action Worksheets' are developed for each client to meet that client's specific needs.

- A management kit is developed for your organisation for the on-going implementation of management skills back in the workplace.

- An implementation and monitoring strategy is developed for use by each participant and their manager for back at work application of skills.

**If you would like to train your managers in the philosophy
and actions of "You lead, they'll follow" ,
phone freecall 1800 1800 42 (within Australia) or
+ (618) 9284 0039 outside Australia or e-mail msi@iexpress.net.au**

Frontline Management Program

Aim

To develop the competence of frontline managers and their managers through a comprehensive learning program with a focus on application in the workplace.

Outcome

Improvement in individual and team performance through better leadership and management of the technical, human and conceptual factors that affect profitability and productivity.

Features

- Based on the latest Frontline Management Competency Standards endorsed by the Australian National Training Authority.
- Nationally accredited course.
- Recognises prior learning.
- Approximately 1 to 2 years duration.
- 11 separate, self-standing, self-paced modules available of 2 days duration (on average) as desired.
- Incorporates workplace projects related to participant's accountabilities.
- Mentored by participant's manager.
- Mentoring workshop for participants' managers.
- Tutorial sessions for each module (action learning/feedback sessions).
- Assessment of workplace projects by mentor and facilitators.
- Can incorporate a 360° assessment process.

You can effect this program through a partnership with Bentley Kehoe Consulting Group who is able to:

- Certify attainment of competence.
- Facilitate the learning.
- Develop the learning resources and workplace projects in consultation with the client.
- Provide a regular, scheduled 'tutorial' service for participants.
- Provide the assessment of the application of learning.

If you would like to find out more about the Frontline Management Program, please phone freecall 1800 1800 42 (within Australia) or + (618) 9284 0039 outside Australia or e-mail msi@iexpress.net.au